Mastering Data Structures *Enhance Your Programming Skills*

A Step-by-Step Guide to Understanding and Implementing Algorithms

MIGUEL FARMER

RAFAEL SANDERS

Table of Content

TABLE OF CONTENTS

INTRODUCTION 8

Mastering Data Structures and Algorithms – A Step-by-Step Guide to Enhancing Your Programming Skills 8

Why This Book? 8

Why Are Data Structures and Algorithms Important? 10

What You Will Learn 12

Real-World Approach 13

How to Use This Book 14

Final Thoughts 15

Chapter 1 16

Introduction to Data Structures and Algorithms 16

Summary of Key Points: 22

Chapter 2 24

Understanding Time and Space Complexity 24

Summary of Key Points: 31

Chapter 3 32

Arrays – The Building Block 32

Summary of Key Points: 39

Chapter 4 40

Linked Lists – Dynamic Data Handling 40

Summary of Key Points: 48

Chapter 5 50

Stacks and Queues – The Power of Order 50

Chapter 6 60

Hash Tables – Efficient Data Access 60

    Summary of Key Points: 68

Chapter 7 70

Trees – Hierarchical Data Representation 70

Chapter 8 81

Binary Search Trees – Fast Lookups 81

Chapter 9 90

Heaps – Priority Queues in Action 90

Chapter 10 100

Graphs – Representing Connections 100

Chapter 11 110

Searching Algorithms – Finding the Needle in the Haystack .. 110

Chapter 12 118

Sorting Algorithms – Organizing Data Efficiently 118

    Summary of Key Points: 127

Chapter 13 129

Divide and Conquer – Breaking Down Problems 129

    Summary of Key Points: 137

Chapter 14 138

Dynamic Programming – Solving Problems Optimally 138

Chapter 15 147

Greedy Algorithms – Taking the Best Immediate Choice 147

Chapter 16 156

Backtracking – Exploring All Possibilities 156

    Summary of Key Points: 164

Chapter 17 166

Advanced Trees – B-Trees and Tries.................................166

Chapter 18..175

Advanced Graph Algorithms – Finding the Shortest Path.......175

    1. Dijkstra's Algorithm 175

    2. Floyd-Warshall Algorithm...............................177

    3. Bellman-Ford Algorithm.................................179

    Real-World Applications: Navigation Systems, Route
    Planning 180

    Time Complexity Analysis 182

    Summary of Key Points:....................................183

Chapter 19..184

Network Flow Algorithms – Managing Data Flow 184

    Max-Flow Min-Cut Theorem..............................184

    Ford-Fulkerson Algorithm.................................185

    Real-World Examples: Data Transmission and Resource
    Allocation...188

    Use Cases in Computer Networks and Transportation 189

    Implementing Algorithms in Practice 190

    Time Complexity Analysis 191

    Summary of Key Points:....................................192

Chapter 20..194

String Algorithms – Mastering Text Processing...................194

    1. Knuth-Morris-Pratt (KMP) Algorithm..............194

    2. Rabin-Karp Algorithm 196

    Applications: Pattern Matching, Text Searching 198

    Time Complexity and Optimizations.....................199

    Summary of Key Points:....................................201

Chapter 21 202

Computational Geometry – Problem Solving in Geometry 202

    Real-World Examples: Collision Detection, GPS Routing
....203

    Basic Problems: Convex Hull, Closest Pair of Points......205

    Applications in Games and Simulations 207

    Time Complexity and Optimizations 208

    Summary of Key Points: 210

Chapter 22 211

Disjoint Set Union (Union-Find) – Grouping Data Efficiently 211

    Real-World Example: Social Networks, Connectivity
Problems 212

    Operations: Find, Union, Path Compression 213

    Applications in Network Connectivity and Kruskal's
Algorithm 216

    Real-World Use Cases 218

    Time Complexity and Optimizations 220

    Summary of Key Points: 220

Chapter 23 222

Amortized Analysis – Analyzing Average Case Performance 222

    Why Use Amortized Analysis? 222

    Summary of Key Points: 229

Chapter 24 231

Bit Manipulation – Working with Bits Efficiently 231

    Summary of Key Points 239

Chapter 25 241

Advanced Algorithm Design Techniques 241

Summary of Key Points 247

Chapter 26 250

Algorithm Optimization – Improving Performance 250

    1. Parallelism 250

    2. Caching 252

    3. Precomputation 253

    Memory Management Techniques 255

    Case Studies: Performance Improvement in Large-Scale
    Systems 257

    Summary of Key Points 259

Chapter 27 260

Putting It All Together – Building Real-World Applications .. 260

    Real-World Example: Building a Recommendation System
    260

    How to Approach Algorithmic Problem-Solving in
    Software Development 264

    Final Thoughts: Becoming an Expert in Algorithmic
    Thinking 266

INTRODUCTION

Mastering Data Structures and Algorithms – A Step-by-Step Guide to Enhancing Your Programming Skills

In today's world of software development, the ability to design efficient, scalable, and optimized algorithms is more important than ever. Whether you are working on a simple app or building large-scale systems, understanding **data structures** and **algorithms** is crucial to solving problems effectively and ensuring that your code runs efficiently. However, mastering algorithms is not just about memorizing solutions—it's about understanding how and when to apply them, optimizing performance, and solving real-world problems with elegance and speed.

This book, **Mastering Data Structures and Algorithms: Enhance Your Programming Skills – A Step-by-Step Guide to Understanding and Implementing Algorithms**, is designed to take you on a comprehensive journey through the core concepts of data structures and algorithms, giving you the tools needed to excel as a software developer and problem solver.

Why This Book?

Data structures and algorithms form the backbone of computer science and software engineering. Whether you are just beginning your programming journey or are a seasoned developer looking to sharpen your skills, this book provides a systematic approach to mastering these critical topics. It is written to be clear and accessible to both beginners and experienced developers, with **real-world examples** and **step-by-step explanations** that make complex concepts easier to understand.

In this book, we will explore the essential **data structures**—from the simplest, like arrays and linked lists, to more advanced structures, such as trees, graphs, and heaps. We'll also dive deep into the **algorithms** that operate on these structures—sorting, searching, dynamic programming, greedy algorithms, and much more.

Through this guide, you will:

1. **Master fundamental data structures**: Understand how arrays, linked lists, trees, stacks, queues, and graphs work, and how to use them effectively.
2. **Learn key algorithms**: Gain knowledge of crucial algorithms such as sorting, searching, shortest path finding, and dynamic programming, and understand how to optimize their performance.

3. **Understand time and space complexity**: Learn the theory of algorithm efficiency and how to analyze the performance of different solutions using Big O notation.

4. **Apply your skills**: Use practical examples, case studies, and coding exercises to solidify your understanding and apply these concepts to real-world problems, such as building a recommendation system or optimizing a network routing algorithm.

Why Are Data Structures and Algorithms Important?

Data structures and algorithms are the foundation of software development because they allow us to **organize and manipulate data efficiently**. Choosing the right data structure and algorithm can make the difference between an application that performs well and one that lags under pressure.

In simple terms, **data structures** are containers that organize and store data in ways that enable us to perform tasks like searching, sorting, and modifying data effectively. Examples include:

*   **Arrays**: Ordered collections of data.
*   **Linked Lists**: Dynamic data structures that allow for efficient insertions and deletions.
*   **Trees**: Hierarchical structures for representing relationships, such as file systems or decision trees.

- **Graphs**: Represent complex networks of relationships, like social networks or web pages.

On the other hand, **algorithms** are the procedures or step-by-step instructions that process this data. From sorting a list to finding the shortest path between two nodes in a graph, algorithms determine how data is manipulated and how quickly it can be processed. The **efficiency** of an algorithm is a key factor in determining the overall performance of a system, especially when handling large amounts of data.

In the real world, data structures and algorithms are used in a wide variety of applications:

- **Search engines** use advanced algorithms to rank results efficiently.
- **Social media platforms** employ algorithms to suggest relevant content.
- **Navigation apps** rely on algorithms to calculate optimal routes in real-time.

As technology continues to evolve and we move toward more complex systems, a solid understanding of data structures and algorithms becomes even more crucial. Being proficient in these concepts will not only help you write better code but also give you a deep understanding of how computers process information, ultimately making you a more capable problem solver.

What You Will Learn

In this book, we will cover a wide range of topics that are essential for mastering data structures and algorithms, including:

1. **Fundamental Data Structures**: Learn about arrays, linked lists, stacks, queues, trees, graphs, and more. Understand their structure, operations, and use cases.

2. **Core Algorithms**: Dive into sorting, searching, graph algorithms, dynamic programming, greedy algorithms, and backtracking. Learn how to approach algorithmic problems and implement efficient solutions.

3. **Time and Space Complexity**: Master Big O notation, and understand how to evaluate the efficiency of algorithms in terms of time and space.

4. **Advanced Techniques**: Learn about more advanced topics like **divide and conquer**, **dynamic programming**, **greedy algorithms**, and **network flow algorithms**, and understand how to apply these techniques to real-world problems.

5. **Practical Applications**: Apply your knowledge to build real-world applications, such as recommendation systems, network routing solutions, and efficient search engines. Learn how to integrate multiple data structures and algorithms into real-world systems.

6. **Optimization Techniques**: Discover techniques for improving the performance of your algorithms, including parallelism, caching, precomputation, and more.

Real-World Approach

Each chapter in this book is designed with a focus on real-world application. By providing practical examples and case studies, we will demonstrate how to implement data structures and algorithms in a way that is directly applicable to solving problems you will encounter in professional software development. These case studies will cover a variety of domains, such as:

- **Building recommendation systems** for e-commerce or content platforms.
- **Optimizing network routing algorithms** for large-scale distributed systems.
- **Developing machine learning algorithms** for data classification and clustering.
- **Improving system performance** with memory management techniques and algorithm optimizations.

By the end of this book, you will have a strong foundation in both the theory and practical application of data structures and algorithms, enabling you to tackle complex software development challenges with confidence.

How to Use This Book

This book is structured in a way that allows you to build your knowledge progressively. You will start with basic concepts and gradually move on to more complex topics. Each chapter includes:

- **Conceptual explanations**: Clear and concise explanations of key concepts and algorithms.
- **Real-world examples**: Practical examples and case studies to demonstrate how these concepts are applied.
- **Code examples**: Working code examples to illustrate algorithm implementations in popular programming languages like Python, Java, and C++.
- **Exercises**: Challenges and exercises at the end of each chapter to help reinforce your understanding and test your skills.
- **Advanced topics**: For those who wish to delve deeper, we provide detailed explanations of more advanced algorithms and techniques.

You can approach this book sequentially or focus on specific topics that interest you. Whether you are preparing for coding interviews, building real-world applications, or just looking to improve your algorithmic thinking, this book will be your guide to mastering data structures and algorithms.

Final Thoughts

Mastering data structures and algorithms is not an overnight task—it requires patience, practice, and a willingness to experiment with different approaches. By understanding the core principles of algorithmic design, data management, and optimization, you will be equipped with the skills needed to tackle some of the most challenging problems in computer science and software development.

This book is designed to empower you to think algorithmically, providing a step-by-step approach to learning and mastering the tools that will make you a more effective programmer. As you progress through each chapter, you will not only understand the theory behind algorithms and data structures but also gain the confidence to implement them in real-world applications.

So, let's dive into the exciting world of data structures and algorithms, and start building the skills that will define you as a problem solver in the world of software development.

Let's get started!

CHAPTER 1

INTRODUCTION TO DATA STRUCTURES AND ALGORITHMS

What are Data Structures and Algorithms?

At the heart of every computer program lies the efficient handling of data and the ability to perform operations on it. Two critical concepts that drive the functionality and performance of applications are **Data Structures** and **Algorithms**.

- **Data Structures**: A data structure is a way of organizing and storing data so that it can be accessed and modified efficiently. Think of it as a container that holds data, but it also dictates how the data can be accessed and manipulated. For example, a simple array or list is a linear data structure, whereas a tree structure can represent hierarchical relationships between data.

  Example: Consider a list of names of all employees in a company. If the data is stored in an array, accessing a name or adding a new name is straightforward. However, if the data is stored in a more complex structure like a binary search tree (BST), we can ensure that we search for a name more efficiently, especially when dealing with large datasets.

- **Algorithms**: An algorithm is a step-by-step procedure or set of rules for solving a specific problem or performing a task. Algorithms are crucial for the efficient processing of data, whether it's sorting a list, finding the shortest path in a graph, or searching for an element in a collection.

  Example: If you have a list of numbers and you want to sort them in ascending order, there are different algorithms you can use, like **Bubble Sort**, **Merge Sort**, or **Quick Sort**, each with different performance characteristics.

Importance in Programming and Real-World Applications

The way data is structured and the algorithms that are used to manipulate it can make a significant impact on the overall performance and usability of software. Data structures and algorithms are the foundation for writing efficient, optimized, and scalable software.

- **Efficiency**: The choice of data structure affects how quickly you can perform operations like searching, inserting, or deleting. Algorithms help in making decisions on how to process the data. The combination of the right data structure and algorithm ensures that your

17

program can handle large volumes of data in a reasonable time frame.

- **Real-World Impact**: From operating systems to social media apps, almost all software solutions rely on algorithms and data structures to function smoothly. For example, a website's search bar needs a fast way to search a large collection of documents, which is made efficient through algorithms like **binary search** and data structures like **hash tables**. Similarly, social media platforms use algorithms to recommend posts based on your interests and activity.

Example: A real-world example is Google Search. The search engine uses a combination of data structures (like inverted indexes) and algorithms (such as PageRank and other ranking algorithms) to return the most relevant search results quickly. Without these, finding information on the internet would take an unimaginable amount of time.

The Relationship Between Algorithms and Performance

Algorithms and performance are tightly coupled. When discussing performance, we generally refer to two main aspects:

- **Time Complexity**: This measures how the runtime of an algorithm increases as the input size grows. Algorithms

18

with better time complexity (e.g., **O(log n)** for binary search) can handle large datasets more efficiently than those with poor time complexities (e.g., **O(n²)** for bubble sort).

Example: Consider searching for an element in a list. If you use linear search (O(n)), you might need to check each element one by one. But if the list is sorted and you use binary search (O(log n)), you can find the element much faster, even in a large list.

- **Space Complexity**: This refers to the amount of memory required by an algorithm to run. Efficient algorithms minimize both time and space usage.

  Example: A sorting algorithm like **Merge Sort** may have a space complexity of O(n) because it requires additional memory for merging sorted sub-arrays, while **Quick Sort** operates in place and may have a space complexity of O(log n).

The relationship between algorithms and performance isn't just about how fast an algorithm runs; it's about finding the balance between efficiency and resource usage.

The Role of Data Structures in Software Design

The choice of data structure can drastically affect the behavior and efficiency of a program. Every software solution requires different operations, such as storing, retrieving, and updating data, and selecting the right data structure for these tasks is critical to building efficient software.

- **Choosing the Right Data Structure**: Understanding different data structures allows developers to choose the best tool for a given task. For example:
    o **Arrays**: Great for storing elements in a linear format and accessing them by index. But, adding or removing items from the middle of the array can be slow.
    o **Linked Lists**: Perfect for cases where you frequently need to insert or delete elements but don't require fast access by index.
    o **Hash Tables**: Best when you need fast lookups, like in a scenario where you store user information and need quick access by user ID.

Example: Suppose you're designing an e-commerce application. For the product catalog, you might use a **hash table** to quickly find products based on product IDs, but for product categories, a **tree structure** might be more

20

useful to represent the hierarchy of categories (e.g., electronics > mobile phones > smartphones).

- **Software Architecture**: The efficiency of data handling affects the overall architecture of a software system. Efficient data structures reduce the need for excessive computation, enabling real-time responses, especially in applications like games, social media, and databases.

Real-World Examples: How Search Engines Work, Social Media Recommendations

- **Search Engines**: Google uses sophisticated algorithms and data structures to index web pages and rank them based on relevance. When you type a query, the system quickly looks up a large database of indexed pages and ranks them by relevance using algorithms like **PageRank**. The data structure here could be a **graph**, with each web page as a node and the links between them as edges.
- **Social Media Recommendations**: Platforms like Facebook or YouTube recommend content based on your preferences and interactions. They use **graphs** (representing users and connections) and **algorithms** (like collaborative filtering) to suggest content that you might like. These algorithms rely heavily on data structures to process and retrieve user behavior data efficiently.

21

o For example, in Facebook's case, the **graph** represents users as nodes, and the edges between them show relationships such as friends, likes, comments, etc. Recommendations are made by analyzing this graph and finding patterns.

o YouTube's recommendation engine relies on machine learning algorithms, which are optimized through data structures that efficiently store and access user activity data (watch history, liked videos, comments, etc.).

Summary of Key Points:

- **Data Structures** are tools for organizing data efficiently, and **Algorithms** are step-by-step methods for processing that data.

- Choosing the right data structure and algorithm is essential for **program performance** and **real-world applications**, especially when dealing with large datasets or complex tasks.

- In **software design**, the correct data structure influences how well a system functions, enabling faster and more efficient operations.

- Real-world examples like **search engines** and **social media recommendations** highlight how data structures and algorithms are implemented at scale to handle and process data quickly, improving user experience.

This chapter sets the stage for diving deeper into each data structure and algorithm, making them tangible through real-world examples. Let me know if you'd like to expand any specific section or need further clarifications!

CHAPTER 2

UNDERSTANDING TIME AND SPACE COMPLEXITY

Big O Notation Explained in Simple Terms

When we talk about **algorithms** and **program performance**, we often refer to **Big O notation**. Big O is a mathematical notation used to describe the **performance** or **complexity** of an algorithm in terms of time (how long it takes to run) and space (how much memory it requires) as the input size grows.

Big O helps us understand the **scalability** of an algorithm, which is essential when dealing with large data sets. It provides a high-level understanding of how an algorithm's runtime or memory usage increases as the input data grows.

- **Big O** expresses the **worst-case scenario** in terms of time or space, giving us a way to compare algorithms by their efficiency.

For example:

- **O(1)**: This means the algorithm takes **constant time**. No matter how large the input is, the runtime is always the

24

same. This is the best-case scenario in terms of time complexity.

- **O(n)**: This means the algorithm's runtime increases linearly with the input size. If you double the input, the time taken to run the algorithm also doubles.

- **O(n²)**: This means the algorithm's runtime increases quadratically with the input size. For example, if you have a nested loop, the time complexity is typically $O(n^2)$, because for each element in the first loop, you loop through all elements in the second loop.

Time Complexity and Space Complexity with Real-World Examples

Time Complexity: This refers to how the time taken by an algorithm grows with the size of the input.

- **Example 1: Sorting Algorithms on a List of Names**
    - **Bubble Sort ($O(n^2)$)**: Bubble sort compares each element in the list with every other element, and it does this for every item in the list. In the worst-case scenario (a reverse-sorted list), it will compare each pair of elements. Hence, the time complexity is $O(n^2)$.

        Real-World Example: Imagine a list of 100 names, and you're sorting them alphabetically. In bubble sort, for each name, you compare it with every other name, which leads to many redundant comparisons, making the algorithm slower as the list grows.

o **Merge Sort (O(n log n))**: Merge sort, on the other hand, divides the list into smaller sublists, sorts them, and then merges them. The time complexity is O(n log n), meaning the algorithm performs much more efficiently as the list size increases. Merge sort breaks the list down into smaller chunks, which are easier to handle.

Real-World Example: Imagine sorting a list of 100 names again, but this time, you use merge sort. Instead of comparing each name with every other name, merge sort breaks the list into halves, sorts them, and merges them together. This process reduces the number of comparisons required, making it faster, especially for larger lists.

Space Complexity: This refers to how the amount of memory used by an algorithm grows with the size of the input.

- **Example 2: Sorting Algorithms and Space Usage**
  o **Quick Sort (O(log n))**: Quick sort is an in-place sorting algorithm, meaning it doesn't require

extra space to store additional data structures. It sorts elements by partitioning them in place. The space complexity for quicksort is O(log n) due to the recursive stack used for dividing the list.

Real-World Example: When you sort a list of names using quicksort, it doesn't require a second list for temporary storage; it manipulates the list in-place, saving memory.

o **Merge Sort (O(n))**: In contrast, merge sort requires additional memory because it creates temporary sublists to store sorted elements before merging them. The space complexity is O(n), meaning that as the list grows, so does the amount of memory used.

Real-World Example: When sorting a list of 100 names using merge sort, additional memory is required to store the sublists while they are being sorted. For larger lists, this extra memory usage becomes more significant.

Best, Worst, and Average Cases

In algorithm analysis, we often talk about **best-case**, **worst-case**, and **average-case** time complexity to give a full picture of how an algorithm behaves under different conditions.

1. **Best Case**: This is the scenario where the algorithm performs the best (i.e., it takes the least time or uses the least space). It usually happens with a favorable input.

   o **Example**: In a **linear search** algorithm, the best case occurs when the element you're searching for is the first element in the list. This results in O(1) time complexity.

2. **Worst Case**: This is the scenario where the algorithm performs the worst, taking the most time or using the most memory. It's the most important case to consider because it helps to ensure the algorithm will work under all conditions.

   o **Example**: In **bubble sort**, the worst-case scenario occurs when the list is sorted in reverse order. The algorithm will have to compare every pair of elements, leading to a time complexity of $O(n^2)$.

3. **Average Case**: The average case considers the expected performance of the algorithm when inputs are random. This is usually harder to calculate, but it gives us a sense of how the algorithm will perform in typical situations.

   o **Example**: In **quick sort**, the average case occurs when the pivot element divides the list approximately in half at each step, resulting in O(n log n) time complexity.

Practical Scenarios: When to Optimize and Why

In real-world applications, you rarely need to optimize every part of your code. The goal is to identify bottlenecks—those parts of the program that consume the most resources—and optimize them for better performance.

When to Optimize:

- **When performance impacts user experience**: If your program's performance is slowing down the user experience (e.g., slow loading times for a website), it's time to optimize.
  - ○ **Example**: If you're building a **real-time chat app**, you need fast message delivery. A **hash table** might be used for quick lookups, as performance is crucial in these types of applications.
- **When dealing with large datasets**: If you're working with large datasets, algorithms that are **O(n²)**, like bubble sort, will become inefficient quickly, and you should consider more efficient alternatives like **merge sort (O(n log n))** or **quick sort**.
- **When memory usage is critical**: In applications running on devices with limited memory (like mobile phones), using algorithms that require excessive memory (like merge sort) may be impractical. Instead, in-place

algorithms like **quick sort** or **heap sort** can help optimize space usage.

Why to Optimize:

- **Scalability**: Optimizing algorithms ensures that your software can scale to handle larger datasets without a significant drop in performance. A small optimization can lead to substantial performance improvements as your dataset grows.
- **Cost Efficiency**: Optimizing algorithms that require fewer resources (like CPU time and memory) can reduce hardware and operational costs, especially for large-scale systems or cloud-based applications.
- **User Satisfaction**: Faster applications and programs with lower memory usage are more efficient and provide a better user experience.

Real-World Optimization Example: Let's say you are building an e-commerce website. The website has a feature that lets users filter products by price, category, and ratings. If the website uses a **linear search** (O(n)) to check each product against the filter criteria, it might be fine for a small number of products. However, as the product list grows, the search will slow down. Optimizing this by using **binary search** (O(log n)) on a sorted list of products could significantly speed up the process, providing a better user experience.

Summary of Key Points:

- **Big O Notation** provides a way to express the time and space complexity of algorithms, making it easier to compare their efficiency.
- **Time Complexity** measures how the execution time of an algorithm grows with the size of the input, and **Space Complexity** measures how much memory the algorithm uses.
- **Best, Worst, and Average Cases** help understand the algorithm's behavior under different scenarios, with the worst-case being the most important for performance.
- **Practical Optimization** should focus on areas where performance bottlenecks occur, especially when working with large datasets, or when real-time or memory-constrained environments are involved.

By understanding these concepts and applying them in real-world applications, you'll be well-equipped to choose the right algorithms and data structures to solve problems efficiently.

CHAPTER 3

ARRAYS – THE BUILDING BLOCK

Basic Array Structure, Initialization, and Use Cases

An **array** is one of the simplest and most commonly used data structures. It is a **linear collection** of elements, each of which is stored in a contiguous block of memory. The elements in an array are typically of the same data type, such as integers, strings, or floats, and can be accessed directly using an index.

- **Structure**: An array has a fixed size, meaning you specify how many elements it will hold when you initialize it. The elements are stored in consecutive memory locations, making it efficient for accessing elements by index.
- **Initialization**: When creating an array, you define its size and type of data it will store. Here's an example in **Python**:

```python
Copy
sales_data = [100, 200, 300, 400, 500]
```

In this example, `sales_data` is an array (or list in Python) that holds five elements representing sales figures.

- **Use Cases**: Arrays are used in a wide variety of applications, especially when the data is of a fixed size or when quick access to elements is needed. They are particularly useful when:
  - You need **random access** to elements.
  - You are working with **sequential data** like a list of days in a month, or ordered data like monthly sales.

Example: If you're storing monthly sales data, an array can store the sales for each month in a fixed-size collection where each element corresponds to a specific month.

Access Patterns and Indexing

One of the biggest advantages of arrays is **direct access** to elements via an **index**. Arrays use **zero-based indexing**, meaning the first element is at index 0, the second at index 1, and so on.

- **Access Patterns**: When working with arrays, the time complexity for accessing an element at a given index is **O(1)** (constant time). This makes arrays very efficient when you need to retrieve or update elements at specific positions.

33

Example: If we have the array `sales_data = [100, 200, 300, 400, 500]`, accessing the sales for the third month (index 2) would look like:

```python
Copy
third_month_sales = sales_data[2]    #
Output: 300
```

- **Indexing**: You can access or update array elements directly using their index. For example, to update the sales of the first month, you would do:

```python
Copy
sales_data[0] = 120  # Update January sales
to 120
```

However, the size of an array is **fixed** when it is initialized. If you try to access an index that is out of bounds (e.g., trying to access `sales_data[10]` in an array of size 5), it will result in an **IndexError**.

Real-World Example: Storing Monthly Sales Data

A practical use case for arrays is **storing monthly sales data** for a business or product. Imagine a company that tracks the sales of a product over the course of a year. Using an array, you can store the data for each month.

34

```
python
Copy
# Array representing monthly sales data for a
year
sales_data = [1500, 1800, 2000, 2100, 2200, 2300,
2500, 2400, 2600, 2700, 2800, 2900]
```

Here, each element in the array represents the sales for one month. The first element (index 0) corresponds to January, the second element (index 1) corresponds to February, and so on.

- **Why use an array?**: Arrays are ideal for this scenario because:
  - The number of months (12) is fixed and known beforehand.
  - You can quickly access any month's sales by referring to its index (e.g., `sales_data[0]` for January or `sales_data[11]` for December).

You can also update the sales data if needed. For instance, if you want to update the sales for March (index 2), you can do:

```
python
Copy
sales_data[2] = 2200   # Update March sales to
2200
```

Common Operations: Insertion, Deletion, Search

Arrays are a fundamental data structure, but their operations are somewhat limited compared to other data structures like linked lists or dynamic arrays. Here's a look at some common operations:

1. **Insertion**: Inserting elements into an array is **not very flexible**, because the size of the array is fixed once it is initialized. In most programming languages, you can't just insert an element in the middle of an array without either:

   o **Shifting** elements to make room, which takes O(n) time.

   o **Resizing the array**, which may involve creating a new array and copying elements.

   Example: If you wanted to insert a new sales figure for an additional month (say for the 13th month), you would need to create a new array to hold 13 elements and copy the old sales data into it.

   ```python
   Copy
   new_sales_data = sales_data + [3000]  # Add a new sales data entry for the 13th month
   ```

   o **Time Complexity**: Inserting an element at the end of an array (if the array has space) is O(1), but inserting at any other position (e.g., in the middle) is O(n) due to the need to shift elements.

2. **Deletion**: Like insertion, deletion in an array is not always straightforward, especially when you need to delete an element from the middle or the front of the array. To delete an element:

   o You must shift the subsequent elements to fill the gap, which takes O(n) time.

   o Alternatively, you can mark the element as deleted (e.g., set it to a special value), but the array's size remains the same.

Example: If you wanted to delete the sales data for March (index 2), you would need to shift all the elements after it:

```python
Copy
del sales_data[2]  # Delete the sales data
for March (index 2)
```

3. **Search**: Searching for an element in an array can be done in a few ways:

   o **Linear Search (O(n))**: If the array is unsorted, you must check each element one by one until you find the target.

   Example: Searching for a specific sales value:

```python
Copy
def linear_search(arr, value):
    for i in range(len(arr)):
        if arr[i] == value:
            return i   # Return the
index of the value
    return -1   # Return -1 if the
value is not found
```

- o **Binary Search (O(log n))**: If the array is sorted, you can use binary search to quickly find an element by repeatedly dividing the array in half.

  Example: If the sales data is sorted, binary search is more efficient:

```python
Copy
# Binary search for a sorted array
def binary_search(arr, value):
    low, high = 0, len(arr) - 1
    while low <= high:
        mid = (low + high) // 2
        if arr[mid] == value:
            return mid
        elif arr[mid] < value:
            low = mid + 1
        else:
```

```
        high = mid - 1
return -1
```

4. **Real-World Example**: Searching for sales data above a certain threshold, say looking for months where sales exceeded 2500. In a large dataset, binary search (O(log n)) is much faster than linear search (O(n)).

Summary of Key Points:

- **Arrays** are fundamental data structures for storing ordered data in a contiguous memory block.

- **Initialization** of an array involves defining its size and type of data, making it useful for scenarios with fixed-size data sets.

- **Accessing elements** in an array is done via indices, offering constant-time access (O(1)).

- **Common operations** include insertion, deletion, and search, though inserting and deleting elements can be inefficient if done frequently in the middle of an array.

- **Real-world examples** like storing monthly sales data illustrate how arrays are used to organize data that requires quick access, making them perfect for fixed datasets with known sizes.

CHAPTER 4

LINKED LISTS – DYNAMIC DATA HANDLING

Difference Between Arrays and Linked Lists

Both **arrays** and **linked lists** are data structures used to store collections of elements, but they differ in how they store and manage data. Understanding the differences between these two structures is crucial for selecting the appropriate one depending on the task at hand.

- **Arrays**:
    - Arrays are **fixed-size** data structures. Once an array is created, its size cannot change. If the array is full and you need more space, you must create a new, larger array and copy the elements.
    - Arrays use **contiguous memory allocation**, meaning that all elements are stored in adjacent memory locations. This allows for **quick access** to elements using indices (i.e., O(1) time complexity for access).
    - However, operations like **insertion** and **deletion** (especially in the middle of the array) can be

inefficient, requiring elements to be shifted (O(n) time complexity).

- **Linked Lists**:
  - o Linked lists, on the other hand, are **dynamic data structures**. They can grow and shrink in size as needed during program execution, making them much more flexible than arrays.
  - o Unlike arrays, linked lists use **non-contiguous memory allocation**, meaning that each element (or **node**) in the list is stored at different memory locations. Each node contains a reference (or pointer) to the next node in the list.
  - o The primary advantage of linked lists is that **insertion** and **deletion** operations are much more efficient than in arrays, especially when working with large datasets, because no elements need to be shifted.

In summary, while arrays are better suited for **random access** and **fast access to elements**, linked lists are more efficient for **dynamic data handling**, where frequent insertions and deletions are required.

Types of Linked Lists: Singly Linked List, Doubly Linked List

Linked lists can come in different types, each with its own characteristics and use cases. The two most common types are **singly linked lists** and **doubly linked lists**.

1. **Singly Linked List**:
    o   A **singly linked list** is a chain of nodes where each node contains two parts:
        ▪   **Data**: The actual element the node stores.
        ▪   **Next Pointer**: A reference to the next node in the list.
    o   In a singly linked list, traversal can only be done in one direction, from the first node (head) to the last node (tail).

    Structure Example:

    ```
    text
    Copy
    Head -> [Data | Next] -> [Data | Next] ->
    [Data | Null]
    ```

    o   **Pros**:
        ▪   Memory-efficient: Each node stores only one pointer (to the next node).
        ▪   Simple structure, easy to implement.
    o   **Cons**:

- Traversal can only be done in one direction.
- No easy way to access previous nodes.

2. **Doubly Linked List**:
   o A **doubly linked list** is similar to a singly linked list but with an additional pointer.
   o Each node contains three parts:
      - **Data**: The element the node stores.
      - **Next Pointer**: A reference to the next node in the list.
      - **Previous Pointer**: A reference to the previous node in the list.
   o This allows traversal in both directions (forward and backward), which can be useful for certain applications like navigating a browser history or implementing a playlist.

Structure Example:

```
text
Copy
Null <- [Prev | Data | Next] <-> [Prev |
Data | Next] <-> [Prev | Data | Next] ->
Null
```

   o **Pros**:
      - Allows traversal in both directions.

43

- Easier deletion of nodes because you have direct access to the previous node.
  o **Cons**:
    - Requires more memory (storing an additional pointer for each node).
    - Slightly more complex to implement and maintain.

Real-World Example: Undo Functionality in Text Editors

One of the classic applications of linked lists is implementing the **undo functionality** in text editors. When a user makes changes to a document, the system needs to keep track of all modifications and allow the user to "undo" to a previous state.

- In a **singly linked list** or **doubly linked list**, each change (such as inserting text, deleting a character, or formatting) is stored in a node. The node points to the previous state, allowing for easy traversal backward through the list of changes.

  Example: In a text editor, each node might store a snapshot of the document before a change was made. When the user presses "undo," the editor simply traverses back through the linked list to the previous snapshot. If a **doubly linked list** is used, the editor can efficiently go backward and forward between changes.

44

Operations: Insertion, Deletion, Searching, Traversal

Linked lists support several key operations that make them a powerful and flexible data structure. Let's look at the four most important operations in detail: **insertion**, **deletion**, **searching**, and **traversal**.

1. **Insertion**:
   - **At the Beginning**: To insert a node at the beginning of the list, we create a new node, set its next pointer to the current head of the list, and then update the head to point to the new node.
   - **At the End**: To insert a node at the end of the list, we traverse the entire list until we reach the last node and then set its next pointer to the new node. For a **doubly linked list**, we also update the previous pointer of the new node to point back to the previous last node.
   - **At a Specific Position**: Inserting at a specific position involves traversing the list to the required index, then adjusting the pointers of the surrounding nodes to include the new node.

   Example: Inserting a new node at the beginning of a singly linked list:

   ```python
   Copy
   ```

```
new_node = Node(data)   # Create new node
new_node.next = head  # Set next pointer to
current head
head = new_node  # Update head to new node
```

2. **Deletion**:

   o **At the Beginning**: To delete the first node, we simply update the head pointer to the second node in the list.

   o **At the End**: To delete the last node, we need to traverse the list to find the second-to-last node, then set its next pointer to `null` (or `None` in Python). In a **doubly linked list**, the previous pointer of the last node needs to be updated as well.

   o **At a Specific Position**: Deletion at a specific position requires traversing the list to find the target node and adjusting the pointers of the surrounding nodes to bypass the node to be deleted.

Example: Deleting the first node in a singly linked list:

```python
Copy
head = head.next   # Update head to the
second node
```

3. **Searching**:

> o   Searching in a linked list involves traversing the list and comparing each node's data to the target value. If the target is found, the index or reference to the node is returned. In the worst case, the search time is O(n), where n is the number of nodes in the list.

Example: Searching for a specific value in a singly linked list:

```python
Copy
def search_linked_list(head, target):
    current = head
    while current:
        if current.data == target:
            return current  # Return the
node if found
        current = current.next
    return None  # Return None if not found
```

4. **Traversal**:

> o   **Traversal** refers to visiting each node in the linked list, one by one, to perform some operation (like printing data or modifying values). In a **singly linked list**, traversal starts at the head and

follows the next pointers until it reaches the end (where the next pointer is null).

o   For **doubly linked lists**, you can traverse in both directions: from the head to the tail and vice versa.

Example: Traversing a singly linked list and printing each node's data:

```python
Copy
def print_linked_list(head):
    current = head
    while current:
        print(current.data)
        current = current.next
```

Summary of Key Points:

- **Linked lists** are dynamic data structures that consist of nodes, where each node stores data and a reference to the next node (and possibly the previous node in a doubly linked list).
- **Singly linked lists** allow traversal in one direction, while **doubly linked lists** allow traversal in both directions, making them more flexible.

- **Common operations** for linked lists include insertion (at the beginning, end, or a specific position), deletion (at the beginning, end, or a specific position), searching, and traversal.

- **Real-world examples** like undo functionality in text editors highlight the power of linked lists in managing dynamic data, especially when frequent modifications are needed.

Linked lists offer a dynamic and flexible alternative to arrays, especially when it comes to handling data that changes frequently or requires efficient insertion and deletion operations.

CHAPTER 5

STACKS AND QUEUES – THE POWER OF ORDER

Understanding LIFO (Last In, First Out) and FIFO (First In, First Out)

Stacks and queues are two fundamental data structures that manage elements in a specific order, using different approaches for adding and removing elements. Both structures provide an efficient way of handling data, but they operate based on different principles of ordering.

1. **LIFO (Last In, First Out) - Stacks**:
   - **Definition**: A **stack** is a data structure that follows the **LIFO** principle, which means that the last element added to the stack is the first one to be removed. You can think of a stack as a stack of plates where you add plates to the top and also remove plates from the top.
   - **Operations**: The two main operations associated with stacks are:
     - **Push**: Add an element to the top of the stack.
     - **Pop**: Remove the element from the top of the stack.

Visual Representation of a Stack (LIFO):

```
text
Copy
Top -> [A] -> [B] -> [C] -> Bottom
```

- o In this example, if we perform a pop operation, **C** (the last element added) will be removed first.

2. **FIFO (First In, First Out) - Queues**:
   - o **Definition**: A **queue** operates on the **FIFO** principle, meaning the first element added to the queue is the first one to be removed. A queue behaves like a line at a checkout counter where the first person in line is the first to be served, and people continue to join the line at the rear.
   - o **Operations**: The primary operations for queues are:
     - ▪ **Enqueue**: Add an element to the rear of the queue.
     - ▪ **Dequeue**: Remove the element from the front of the queue.

Visual Representation of a Queue (FIFO):

```
text
Copy
Front -> [A] -> [B] -> [C] -> Rear
```

o In this example, if we perform a dequeue operation, **A** (the first element added) will be removed first.

Real-World Examples: Undo Operations, Task Scheduling

Both stacks and queues have practical applications in various fields like **undo operations** in text editors and **task scheduling** in operating systems.

1. **Undo Operations (Stack - LIFO)**:
   o **Real-World Example**: Most text editors (like Microsoft Word or Google Docs) provide an "undo" feature that allows users to reverse their last action. This functionality is implemented using a **stack**. Each change made by the user is pushed onto a stack. When the user presses "undo," the most recent action (the last pushed item) is popped off the stack, and the editor reverts to that state.
      ▪ For instance, if you type a word and then delete it, the stack will first store the typed word and then the deletion. Pressing undo will pop the deletion action, restoring the word.

   Operations in Undo:

- **Push**: Each user action (e.g., typing a letter, deleting text) is added to the stack.
- **Pop**: The most recent action is undone by popping it off the stack.

2. **Task Scheduling (Queue - FIFO)**:

   o **Real-World Example**: In operating systems, task scheduling is often managed using a **queue**. Jobs or processes are placed in a queue in the order they arrive. The operating system then dequeues the tasks one by one, executing them in the same order in which they were added (i.e., FIFO). This ensures that tasks are processed in the order they were requested.

   - For example, consider print jobs in a printer queue. The first print job sent to the printer will be printed first, and the next job will be printed only after the first job is completed, and so on.

   Operations in Task Scheduling:

   - **Enqueue**: New tasks are added to the rear of the queue.
   - **Dequeue**: Tasks are removed from the front of the queue and processed by the system.

Operations on Stacks and Queues

1. **Stack Operations**:

   o **Push**: To add an element to the stack, we use the **push** operation.

   Example: Adding an item to the stack:

   ```python
   Copy
   stack = []
   stack.append("A")   # Push A onto the stack
   stack.append("B")   # Push B onto the stack
   stack.append("C")   # Push C onto the stack
   ```

   After these operations, the stack looks like:

   ```text
   Copy
   Top -> [C] -> [B] -> [A] -> Bottom
   ```

   o **Pop**: To remove an element from the stack, we use the **pop** operation. This removes the last element added to the stack.

   Example: Removing an item from the stack:

```python
Copy
popped_item = stack.pop()  # Pops "C"
from the stack
```

After the pop operation, the stack becomes:

```text
Copy
Top -> [B] -> [A] -> Bottom
```

o **Peek**: A common additional operation in stacks is **peek**, which allows you to look at the top element without removing it.

Example:

```python
Copy
top_item = stack[-1]  # Peek the top
item ("B")
```

2. **Queue Operations**:

o **Enqueue**: To add an element to the queue, we use the **enqueue** operation, which adds the element to the rear of the queue.

Example: Adding an item to the queue:

```python
```

```
Copy
queue = []
queue.append("A")    # Enqueue A into
the queue
queue.append("B")    # Enqueue B into
the queue
queue.append("C")    # Enqueue C into
the queue
```

After these operations, the queue looks like:

```
text
Copy
Front -> [A] -> [B] -> [C] -> Rear
```

o **Dequeue**: To remove an element from the queue, we use the **dequeue** operation. This removes the first element from the front of the queue.

Example: Removing an item from the queue:

```
python
Copy
dequeued_item = queue.pop(0)    #
Dequeue "A" from the queue
```

After the dequeue operation, the queue becomes:

```
text
Copy
```

```
Front -> [B] -> [C] -> Rear
```

o **Front**: Another common operation is to look at the front element without removing it, which can be done using **front**.

Example:

```python
Copy
front_item = queue[0]    # Peek the
front item ("B")
```

Use Cases in Real-World Applications

1. **Web Browsers (Stack - LIFO)**:
   o Web browsers like Chrome or Firefox use a **stack** to manage the back and forward buttons. Every time a user visits a page, the URL is pushed onto the stack. When the user presses the "back" button, the browser pops the most recent URL from the stack and takes the user to that page.

2. **CPU Scheduling (Queue - FIFO)**:
   o In operating systems, **CPU scheduling** can be done using a **queue**. When processes arrive in the system, they are placed in a queue and scheduled for execution in the order they arrive. This ensures fair and predictable task execution.

3. **Function Call Stack (Stack - LIFO)**:

o   In programming, the function call stack works on the LIFO principle. Each time a function is called, it is pushed onto the stack. When the function finishes executing, it is popped off the stack, and control is returned to the previous function.

4. **Printing Jobs (Queue - FIFO)**:

o   In a **printer queue**, print jobs are added in the order they are received. The first job that enters the queue is the first one to be printed, following the FIFO principle.

Summary of Key Points:

- **Stacks** follow the **LIFO** principle, where the last element added is the first one to be removed. They are ideal for situations like undo operations or tracking function calls in programming.
- **Queues** follow the **FIFO** principle, where the first element added is the first one to be removed. They are useful for task scheduling, managing print jobs, or serving requests in the order they are received.
- Common operations for stacks include **push**, **pop**, and **peek**, while for queues, they include **enqueue**, **dequeue**, and **front**.
- Real-world applications, such as **web browsers**, **CPU scheduling**, and **printing systems**, rely heavily on stacks

and queues to maintain order and manage tasks efficiently.

CHAPTER 6

HASH TABLES – EFFICIENT DATA ACCESS

How Hash Tables Work (Hashing, Collisions, Buckets)

A **hash table** is a highly efficient data structure used to store key-value pairs, enabling **fast access**, **insertion**, and **deletion** of elements. It uses a special function called a **hash function** to map keys to specific locations (or **buckets**) in an underlying array or list. This makes data retrieval very quick compared to other data structures like arrays or linked lists, where searching may require traversing the entire structure.

1. **Hashing**:
   - **Hashing** is the process of converting a key (which can be a string, integer, or any other data type) into a fixed-size index or location in an array. This is done by passing the key through a **hash function**. The hash function computes an integer index based on the key, which determines where the data is stored in the array.

   Example: For a key "apple", a hash function might convert it into an integer like hash("apple") = 3, meaning the value associated with "apple" will be stored in bucket 3 of the hash table.

2. **Collisions**:

   o **Collisions** occur when two different keys hash to the same index or bucket. Since each bucket in the hash table can only hold one value, a collision requires a mechanism to handle the conflict.

   Common techniques for handling collisions include:

   o **Chaining**: Each bucket contains a linked list (or another collection), and all elements that hash to the same bucket are stored in that list. When a collision happens, the new element is simply added to the linked list.

   o **Open Addressing**: If a collision occurs, the hash table searches for the next available bucket using a specific probing technique (e.g., linear probing, quadratic probing).

3. **Buckets**:

   o **Buckets** are essentially the containers in the hash table where the data is stored. In an array-based hash table, each bucket is an index in the array, and the hash function determines which index to use. If multiple keys map to the same bucket (i.e., a collision), the bucket stores the values using chaining or open addressing.

Example of a Hash Table (with collision handling through chaining):

```text
Copy
Index: 0   1    2    3    4
Bucket: [ ]  [ ]  ["apple" → "fruit"]  [ ]
["banana" → "fruit"]
```

In this example, `"apple"` and `"banana"` might hash to different indices, but if two keys map to the same bucket, we store them in a chain (linked list) within the bucket.

Real-World Examples: Dictionary Lookups, Caching

Hash tables are widely used in various real-world applications due to their fast access times. Two common use cases are **dictionary lookups** and **caching**.

1. **Dictionary Lookups**:
    o   A **dictionary** (or **map**) is a common data structure where you store pairs of keys and values. In many programming languages, dictionaries are implemented using hash tables.

62

o For instance, when you look up a word in an English dictionary, the word (key) is hashed into a position where the definition (value) is stored. Hash tables allow the dictionary to quickly find the definition of a word, even if the dictionary contains millions of words.

Example: In Python, the dict type is implemented using a hash table. If you want to look up the definition of a word, Python's dictionary performs a **hash lookup**, which is typically O(1) in average time complexity.

```python
Copy
dictionary = {"apple": "a fruit", "banana": "another fruit"}
print(dictionary["apple"])    # Output: a fruit
```

2. **Caching**:

o **Caching** is another real-world application where hash tables are commonly used. In caching, frequently accessed data (like web pages or database query results) is stored in memory for fast retrieval. Hash tables enable fast lookups of cached data, improving the performance of systems.

63

o   When a request is made for data, the cache checks if the data already exists. If it does, the cached data is returned. If not, the data is computed or fetched from the source and added to the cache.

Example: A web server might cache the result of a complex database query. The query parameters (like user ID) are used as keys, and the query result is stored as the value in the hash table. When the same query is requested again, the server can return the cached result in constant time (O(1)) instead of querying the database.

Example of caching using a hash table:

```python
Copy
cache = {}
def fetch_data_from_cache(query):
    if query in cache:
        return  cache[query]    #  Return
cached result
    else:
        result = fetch_data(query)  # Fetch
from original source
        cache[query] = result  # Cache the
result for future lookups
        return result
```

Operations on Hash Tables: Insert, Search, Delete

The efficiency of hash tables lies in their ability to perform common operations like **insertion, searching,** and **deletion** very quickly. Let's break down each of these operations:

1. **Insert**:

    o   To insert an element into a hash table, you first compute the hash of the key. This determines which bucket the element will go into. If there's a collision, the chosen collision resolution method (e.g., chaining or open addressing) is used.

    Example: Inserting a key-value pair into a hash table with chaining:

```python
Copy
def insert(hash_table, key, value):
    index = hash(key) % len(hash_table)  # Get bucket index using hash function
    if hash_table[index] is None:
        hash_table[index] = [(key, value)]
    else:
        hash_table[index].append((key, value))  # Chaining: Add to the list
```

2. **Search**:

o Searching in a hash table starts by hashing the key to determine the appropriate bucket. If the key exists in that bucket, the corresponding value is returned. In the case of collisions, the search proceeds through the chain (in chaining) or via probing (in open addressing).

Example: Searching for a value using a hash table:

```python
Copy
def search(hash_table, key):
    index = hash(key) % len(hash_table)
    if hash_table[index] is None:
        return None   # Key not found
    else:
        for item in hash_table[index]:
            if item[0] == key:
                return item[1]   # Return value
        return None   # Key not found
```

3. **Delete**:

o Deleting an element from a hash table involves finding the appropriate bucket using the hash function. Once found, the element is either removed from the bucket or the link in the chain is adjusted (for chaining).

Example: Deleting an element from a hash table:

```python
Copy
def delete(hash_table, key):
    index = hash(key) % len(hash_table)
    if hash_table[index] is not None:
        for i, item in enumerate(hash_table[index]):
            if item[0] == key:
                del hash_table[index][i]
                # Remove the key-value pair
                return True
    return False  # Key not found
```

Use in Applications Like Databases and Web Server Caching

Hash tables are widely used in applications where efficient data retrieval is critical. Some common use cases include:

1. **Databases**:
   - **Hashing** is often used in database indexing to speed up query execution. Instead of searching through all records, a hash table allows for quick lookups of records based on a key (such as an ID).
   - For instance, databases like **MySQL** and **PostgreSQL** use hash indexes for fast retrieval of records. The primary key of a table is often stored in a hash table for fast access.

2. **Web Server Caching**:

    o   **Caching** frequently accessed content (such as web pages or API responses) using a hash table enables a web server to deliver responses much faster. Hash keys are typically based on the URL or query parameters, and the corresponding value is the cached result.

    Example: When a user requests a page, the web server checks if the page is in the cache using a hash table. If the page is found, it's returned immediately; otherwise, the page is generated and stored in the cache for future requests.

Summary of Key Points:

- **Hash tables** are powerful data structures that allow fast access to data using a **hash function** to map keys to indices in an array of **buckets**.
- **Collisions** are handled using techniques like **chaining** or **open addressing** to store multiple elements in the same bucket.
- Real-world examples like **dictionary lookups** and **caching** show how hash tables are used in applications to speed up data retrieval and improve system performance.

68

- Key operations in hash tables include **insertion**, **searching**, and **deletion**, each of which can be performed efficiently with an average time complexity of **O(1)**.

- **Databases** and **web server caching** rely on hash tables to manage and retrieve large amounts of data quickly and efficiently.

CHAPTER 7

TREES – HIERARCHICAL DATA REPRESENTATION

Introduction to Tree Structures (Binary Trees, Binary Search Trees)

A **tree** is a hierarchical data structure that consists of **nodes** connected by **edges**. It is one of the most powerful data structures used to represent data with a hierarchical relationship, such as organizational structures, file systems, and decision trees. A tree has a **root node**, from which all other nodes (known as **child nodes**) branch out, forming a tree-like structure.

1. **Binary Trees**:
    - A **binary tree** is a tree data structure where each node has at most **two child nodes**. These child nodes are typically referred to as the **left** child and the **right** child. A binary tree can be used to represent hierarchical data where each node has two possible options or decisions to make.

   Structure of a Binary Tree:

   ```
   text
   Copy
       Root
   ```

```
  /  \
Left  Right
 /      \
Left2   Right2
```

- o In a binary tree, there are no specific rules about the arrangement of values; the left and right children can contain any data.

2. **Binary Search Trees (BST):**

- o A **binary search tree (BST)** is a specific type of binary tree where **the left child node contains values less than the parent node**, and **the right child node contains values greater than the parent node**. This ordering property allows for efficient searching, insertion, and deletion operations.

Structure of a Binary Search Tree:

```
text
Copy
      10
     /  \
    5    15
   / \   / \
  2  7 12  20
```

- o In this example, for every node, values in the left subtree are smaller, and values in the right subtree are larger. This ensures that **searching** for a value can be done efficiently, as you can eliminate half of the tree at each step by following the left or right child based on the comparison.

Real-World Examples: File System Directory Structures

One of the most intuitive real-world examples of tree structures is a **file system directory structure**. The file system on a computer is inherently hierarchical, with folders containing files or other subfolders.

- **Root**: The main directory (e.g., C:\ on Windows or / on Linux) serves as the root of the file system.
- **Nodes**: Each directory or file is a node.
- **Children**: Directories can contain other directories or files as child nodes.

For example:

```
text
Copy
Root
    ├── Documents
    │   ├── Work
    │   └── Personal
    ├── Pictures
    └── Music
```

In this example, the root directory contains **Documents**, **Pictures**, and **Music** as child nodes. The **Documents** node further contains child directories like **Work** and **Personal**. This hierarchical structure allows for easy organization and efficient navigation through files and directories.

Traversal Methods: Pre-order, In-order, Post-order

Traversal refers to visiting every node in the tree and performing a specific operation on each node (such as printing its value). There are several common ways to traverse a tree, especially binary trees. These include **pre-order**, **in-order**, and **post-order** traversals. The order in which the nodes are visited differentiates these methods.

1. **Pre-order Traversal**:
   - In pre-order traversal, the node is **visited first**, then its left child is recursively visited, and then its right child is recursively visited.
   - **Pre-order** is useful when you want to process the root node before its children, for example, when copying a tree structure.

Pre-order Traversal Steps:

3. Visit the current node.
4. Traverse the left subtree.
5. Traverse the right subtree.

Example:

```
text
Copy
Tree:
     10
    /  \
   5    15
  / \   / \
 2   7 12   20
```

Pre-order: 10, 5, 2, 7, 15, 12, 20

2. **In-order Traversal**:

- o In in-order traversal, the **left subtree is visited first**, then the current node is visited, and finally, the right subtree is visited.

- o **In-order** traversal is especially useful for **binary search trees (BST)** because it visits the nodes in ascending order, thus providing a sorted list of values.

In-order Traversal Steps:

2. Traverse the left subtree.
3. Visit the current node.
4. Traverse the right subtree.

Example:

74

```
text
Copy
Tree:
     10
    /  \
   5     15
  / \   / \
 2   7 12  20
```

```
In-order: 2, 5, 7, 10, 12, 15, 20
```

3. **Post-order Traversal**:

- o In post-order traversal, both **left and right subtrees are visited first**, and the current node is visited last.

- o **Post-order** is often used in scenarios like **deleting a tree**, where the children must be deleted before the parent.

Post-order Traversal Steps:

2. Traverse the left subtree.

3. Traverse the right subtree.

4. Visit the current node.

Example:

```
text
Copy
```

75

```
Tree:
     10
    /  \
   5    15
  / \   / \
 2   7 12  20
```

Post-order: 2, 7, 5, 12, 20, 15, 10

Operations: Insertion, Deletion, Searching

Trees, and especially **binary search trees**, provide efficient ways to perform common operations like **insertion, deletion,** and **searching**.

1. **Insertion**:
   - o In a binary tree, insertion is done by finding the correct location for the new node. If it's a binary search tree, the insertion will follow the rule where nodes with smaller values go to the left of the parent, and nodes with larger values go to the right.

Insertion in a Binary Search Tree:

   - o Start at the root.
   - o Compare the new value with the current node.
   - o If the new value is smaller, move to the left child.
   - o If the new value is larger, move to the right child.

76

o Repeat until you find an empty spot (i.e., a null child) and insert the new node there.

Example: Inserting 13 into the tree:

```
text
Copy
    10
   /  \
  5    15
 / \  /  \
2   7 12  20


After inserting 13:
    10
   /  \
  5    15
 / \  /  \
2   7 12  20
         /
        13
```

2. **Deletion**:

o Deleting a node from a binary search tree involves three cases:

1. **Node is a leaf** (no children): Simply remove the node.

2. **Node has one child**: Remove the node and replace it with its child.

3. **Node has two children**: Find the **in-order successor** (the smallest node in the right subtree) or the **in-order predecessor** (the largest node in the left subtree), replace the node with this successor or predecessor, and then delete the successor or predecessor.

Example: Deleting 5 from the tree:

```
text
Copy
    10
   /  \
  5    15
 / \   / \
2   7 12  20


After deleting 5:
    10
   /  \
  7    15
 /     / \
2     12  20
```

3. **Searching**:
   - Searching for a value in a tree can be done by following the same approach as insertion.

Starting from the root, you compare the target value with the current node:

- If the target is smaller, move to the left child.
- If the target is larger, move to the right child.
- If you find the target, you return the node; if you reach a null node, the target doesn't exist in the tree.

Example: Searching for 7 in the tree:

```text
Copy
10
```

```
/
5            15            /            \            /
2 7 12 20
```

```pgsql
Copy
```

```
Starting from the root (10), since 7 is smaller,
you move left. Then, at node 5, since 7 is larger,
you move right and find the target node.
```

79

Summary of Key Points:

- **Trees** are hierarchical data structures consisting of nodes with **parent-child** relationships, where each node can have zero, one, or two child nodes.

- **Binary trees** allow for two children per node, while **binary search trees (BSTs)** enforce an ordering rule that enables efficient searching and insertion.

- **Real-world examples** like file system directories demonstrate how trees can be used to represent hierarchical data, with directories containing subdirectories or files as child nodes.

- **Traversal methods** (pre-order, in-order, and post-order) are used to visit nodes in different orders, depending on the use case.

- Key operations in trees include **insertion**, **deletion**, and **searching**, all of which can be done efficiently in a **binary search tree**.

CHAPTER 8

BINARY SEARCH TREES – FAST LOOKUPS

How Binary Search Trees Work

A **Binary Search Tree (BST)** is a special type of binary tree where each node follows a specific ordering rule. The **left child** of a node must contain a value **less than** the parent node, and the **right child** must contain a value **greater than** the parent node. This ordering property allows for **efficient searching, insertion**, and **deletion** operations, which can be done much faster than other data structures like arrays or linked lists.

Key Properties of a Binary Search Tree:

1. **Left Subtree**: All values in the left subtree of a node are smaller than the node's value.

2. **Right Subtree**: All values in the right subtree of a node are larger than the node's value.

3. **Search Efficiency**: Searching in a BST works by comparing the target value to the current node:

   o   If the target is smaller, the search moves to the **left** child.

o If the target is larger, the search moves to the **right** child.

o This continues recursively until the target is found or the search reaches a leaf node (null).

Example of a Binary Search Tree:

text
Copy

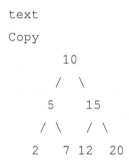

```
      10
     /  \
    5    15
   / \   / \
  2   7 12  20
```

In this example:

- The root node (10) has **5** as its left child (which is smaller than 10) and **15** as its right child (which is greater than 10).
- The left subtree of 10 follows the rule, with nodes **2** and **7** being smaller than 10, and the right subtree has nodes **12** and **20** which are larger than 10.

Operations on Binary Search Trees:

- **Search**: The search process in a BST is efficient. Starting from the root, you compare the target value with the current node and move either left or right, reducing the

82

number of nodes to search at each step. This results in an **O(log n)** time complexity for search in a balanced BST.

- **Insert**: Insertion follows the same process as search: starting from the root, you find the correct position in the tree by comparing values, then insert the new node at that position.

- **Delete**: Deletion is a bit more involved, especially when the node to be deleted has two children. It typically involves finding the **in-order successor** or **in-order predecessor**, which is the smallest node in the right subtree or the largest node in the left subtree.

Real-World Example: Efficient Searching in Large Data Sets

One of the best real-world applications of a Binary Search Tree is in **efficient searching** within large datasets. Consider a **library catalog** system where the books are identified by their **ISBN numbers** or **book titles**.

- If the library stores the book catalog as an **unsorted list**, searching for a book would require checking every entry one by one, resulting in **O(n)** time complexity.

- By using a **Binary Search Tree (BST)**, however, the catalog can be stored in a way that allows for fast searches. When searching for a book, you start at the root and compare the ISBN number or book title with the current node. Based on the comparison, you move left or

83

right, progressively narrowing down the search. This results in an **O(log n)** search time in a balanced BST.

Example: A library catalog of 1,000,000 books:

- **Unsorted List**: If you search for a book in an unsorted list, you may need to check every entry (O(n) time).
- **BST**: If the books are stored in a BST, you can find the book in just **log(1,000,000)** comparisons (around 20 comparisons), making searching significantly faster.

Balanced vs. Unbalanced Trees

The performance of a Binary Search Tree depends heavily on its **balance**. If a BST becomes **unbalanced**, its performance can degrade significantly.

1. **Balanced Tree**:
   - In a balanced BST, the height of the left and right subtrees of any node differs by at most 1. This ensures that the tree remains relatively shallow, and operations like search, insertion, and deletion can be performed in **O(log n)** time.
   - A balanced tree ensures that each level of the tree is populated as evenly as possible, which minimizes the depth and maximizes the search efficiency.

Example of a Balanced Tree:

```text
Copy
     10
    /  \
   5    15
  / \   / \
 2   7 12  20
```

In this tree, the left and right subtrees of each node are balanced, and the height of the tree is minimal.

2. **Unbalanced Tree**:
   o An unbalanced tree occurs when elements are inserted in a non-optimal order, causing the tree to lean heavily in one direction (like a linked list).
   o In the worst case, a Binary Search Tree can become a **degenerate tree** (essentially a linked list), where all nodes are either to the left or right of each other. This results in **O(n)** time complexity for operations, which defeats the purpose of using a BST in the first place.

Example of an Unbalanced Tree:

```text
Copy
     10
```

```
    \
    15
      \
      20
        \
        25
```

This tree is unbalanced and behaves like a linked list. Searching for a value like **25** will require **O(n)** comparisons, which is inefficient.

Rotations and Balancing Techniques (AVL Trees, Red-Black Trees)

To ensure that a Binary Search Tree remains balanced and provides **O(log n)** performance for all operations, various **balancing techniques** have been developed. These techniques use **rotations** to maintain balance whenever the tree becomes unbalanced due to insertions or deletions.

1. **Rotations**:
   - A **rotation** is an operation that changes the structure of the tree without changing the order of the elements. There are two types of rotations:
     - **Left Rotation**: The left child of a node becomes the new parent, and the original parent becomes the left child of the new parent.

- **Right Rotation**: The right child of a node becomes the new parent, and the original parent becomes the right child of the new parent.

Example of a Right Rotation:

text
Copy

```
    10                    15
   / \                   / \
  5   15    ->     10       20
```

In this case, a right rotation on the node 10 makes 15 the new root, maintaining the BST properties.

2. **AVL Trees (Adelson-Velsky and Landis Tree)**:
   - An **AVL tree** is a self-balancing binary search tree where the height difference (or **balance factor**) between the left and right subtrees of any node is at most **1**. If the balance factor exceeds 1 or -1 after an insertion or deletion, the tree is rebalanced using rotations.
   - The height of an AVL tree is always **O(log n)**, which ensures that all operations remain efficient.

Example of AVL Tree Balance Factor:

text

```
Copy
Balance Factor = Height of Left Subtree -
Height of Right Subtree
```

3. **Red-Black Trees**:
   o A **Red-Black tree** is another type of self-balancing binary search tree. In addition to the binary search tree properties, Red-Black trees enforce additional rules that ensure the tree remains balanced:
     ▪ Every node is either **red** or **black**.
     ▪ The root is always **black**.
     ▪ Red nodes cannot have red children (i.e., no two red nodes can be adjacent).
     ▪ Every path from a node to its descendant null nodes must have the same number of black nodes.

   Red-Black trees are not perfectly balanced but are **approximately balanced**, ensuring that the tree's height is **O(log n)**, leading to efficient search, insert, and delete operations.

Summary of Key Points:

- A **Binary Search Tree (BST)** is a tree structure where nodes follow a strict order: the left child is smaller, and the right child is larger than the parent node, which allows for **efficient searching, insertion**, and **deletion**.

- **Balanced trees** ensure that the height of the tree remains minimal, leading to efficient operations with time complexity **O(log n)**.

- **Unbalanced trees** can degrade into linked lists, where operations take **O(n)** time.

- **Rotations** and balancing techniques, such as **AVL trees** and **Red-Black trees**, maintain the balance of the tree, ensuring that all operations remain efficient even after frequent insertions and deletions.

CHAPTER 9

HEAPS – PRIORITY QUEUES IN ACTION

How Heaps Work and Types (Min-Heap, Max-Heap)

A **heap** is a special type of binary tree used to implement **priority queues**, where each node follows a specific order that allows quick access to the **highest** or **lowest** priority element. In a heap, the **parent nodes** must follow certain rules when compared to their **child nodes**, making heaps very efficient for operations like insertion, deletion, and accessing the root element.

Heaps can be classified into two types:

1. **Min-Heap**:
    - o In a **min-heap**, the **value of each parent node is less than or equal to** the values of its children. This ensures that the **smallest element** is always at the **root** of the tree, allowing quick access to the minimum element.
    - o **Min-heap properties**:
        - The root node has the minimum value.
        - The left and right subtrees of any node must also be heaps (min-heaps).

Example of a Min-Heap:

```
text
Copy
      3
     / \
    5   8
   / \ / \
  9 10 12  15
```

In this min-heap:

- o The root is **3**, the smallest element.
- o Each parent node (e.g., 5) is less than or equal to its children (e.g., 9, 10).

2. **Max-Heap**:
   - o In a **max-heap**, the **value of each parent node is greater than or equal to** the values of its children. This ensures that the **largest element** is always at the **root**, allowing quick access to the maximum element.
   - o **Max-heap properties**:
     - ▪ The root node has the maximum value.
     - ▪ The left and right subtrees of any node must also be heaps (max-heaps).

Example of a Max-Heap:

```
text
```

```
Copy
      15
     /  \
   10    12
   / \  / \
  8   5 9  7
```

In this max-heap:

- The root is **15**, the largest element.
- Each parent node (e.g., 10) is greater than or equal to its children (e.g., 8, 5).

Real-World Example: Job Scheduling, Priority-Based Tasks

One of the most common real-world uses of heaps is in **job scheduling** and **priority-based task management**.

1. **Job Scheduling**:
   - In operating systems, tasks or jobs that require execution can be managed using a **priority queue** implemented with a heap. The tasks are assigned a **priority level**, and the system always selects the highest-priority job to execute next.
   - For example, in a **min-heap**, the job with the smallest priority value (highest priority) is always at the root. In a **max-heap**, the job with the largest

priority value (highest priority) would be at the root.

Example: Consider a scenario where several jobs need to be processed based on their priority levels:

```
text
Copy
Job Priority:
Job A -> Priority 1 (highest)
Job B -> Priority 3
Job C -> Priority 2
```

Using a **min-heap**, **Job A** (priority 1) will always be selected first for processing. The heap automatically ensures that the highest priority job is always efficiently accessible.

2. **Priority-Based Tasks**:
   o A **priority queue** can also be used in **real-time systems** (such as routers or schedulers) where tasks with higher priority must be processed before lower priority tasks. For instance, in **network packet scheduling**, higher-priority packets are handled before lower-priority ones to ensure timely delivery.

Example: A network router might use a **max-heap** to prioritize packets for delivery. The highest priority packet is always at the root and is dequeued for transmission first.

Operations: Insert, Delete, Heapify

Heaps provide several key operations that allow for efficient management of data:

1. **Insert**:
   - Inserting an element into a heap involves adding the element at the **end** of the heap (i.e., the last position in the tree). After inserting, the heap property must be restored by **bubbling up** the element (comparing it with its parent and swapping if necessary).

   Example: Inserting a value into a min-heap:

   - Suppose you want to insert **4** into the following min-heap:

```text
Copy
      3
     / \
    5   8
   / \ / \
  9 10 12  15
```

o   Insert **4** at the end:

text
Copy
```
      3
     / \
    5   8
   / \ / \ 4
  9  10 12   15
```

o   Then, **bubble up** the value **4** to maintain the heap property:

text
Copy
```
      3
     / \
    4   8
   / \ / \
  9  5 12   15
```

2. **Delete**:

o   Deleting an element from a heap typically involves removing the **root node** (the highest priority element). After removing the root, the last element in the heap is moved to the root, and the heap property is restored by **bubbling down** (comparing the new root with its children and

95

swapping it with the smaller/larger child to maintain the heap property).

Example: Deleting the root from the above min-heap:

o Remove the root **3** and move the last element **15** to the root:

```text
Copy
      15
     /  \
    5    8
   / \  / \
  9  10 12
```

o Then, **bubble down** the value **15** to restore the heap property:

```text
Copy
       5
      /  \
     9    8
    / \  / \
  15   10 12
```

3. **Heapify**:

o The **heapify** operation is used to convert an unsorted array into a valid heap. It works by repeatedly applying the **bubble down** operation to ensure that the tree satisfies the heap property.

o **Heapify** can be applied in two scenarios:

  ▪ **Building a heap**: Given an unordered array, heapify rearranges it into a valid heap.

  ▪ **Heapify down**: When removing an element or adjusting the heap, the heap property is restored by moving elements down the tree.

Example: Heapifying an unsorted array [5, 9, 3, 7, 2, 8] into a min-heap:

o Starting with the array, heapify the elements to ensure that the smallest element is always at the root.

```
text
Copy
Initial Array: [5, 9, 3, 7, 2, 8]
After Heapify: [2, 5, 3, 7, 9, 8]
```

Now, the array is rearranged into a valid min-heap.

Use in Algorithms Like Heap Sort

Heaps are often used in algorithms like **heap sort**, which is an efficient comparison-based sorting algorithm. Heap sort works by repeatedly removing the root node (the maximum or minimum value, depending on the heap type) from the heap and placing it into the sorted array.

Heap Sort Algorithm:

1. **Build a heap** from the input data.
2. Repeatedly remove the root node (the highest or lowest value) from the heap and place it into the array.
3. Restore the heap property after each removal.
4. The array is now sorted.

Example of Heap Sort:

```text
Copy
Unsorted Array: [5, 9, 3, 7, 2, 8]
1. Build Min-Heap: [2, 5, 3, 7, 9, 8]
2. Remove root (2): [3, 5, 8, 7, 9] (heapify)
3. Remove root (3): [5, 7, 8, 9] (heapify)
4. Continue until the heap is empty.
Sorted Array: [2, 3, 5, 7, 8, 9]
```

- **Time Complexity**: Heap sort has a time complexity of **O(n log n)**, making it efficient for large datasets, especially compared to simpler algorithms like **bubble sort (O(n²))**.

Summary of Key Points:

- **Heaps** are specialized binary trees used to implement **priority queues**, where elements are stored in a specific order (min-heap or max-heap).

- **Min-heaps** give quick access to the smallest element, while **max-heaps** give quick access to the largest element.

- Real-world applications of heaps include **job scheduling** and **priority-based task management**, ensuring that higher-priority tasks are processed first.

- Common operations in heaps include **insert, delete**, and **heapify**, all of which are efficient with **O(log n)** time complexity.

- **Heap sort** is a well-known algorithm that uses heaps to sort data in **O(n log n)** time.

CHAPTER 10

GRAPHS – REPRESENTING CONNECTIONS

Introduction to Graphs (Directed, Undirected, Weighted, Unweighted)

A **graph** is a data structure used to represent **connections** between entities. Graphs consist of two primary components:

- **Nodes (or vertices)**: Represent entities or objects in the graph.
- **Edges (or links)**: Represent the relationships or connections between nodes.

Graphs can be classified based on the following characteristics:

1. **Directed vs. Undirected Graphs**:
   - o **Directed Graph (Digraph)**: In a directed graph, each edge has a **direction**. An edge from node A to node B means that the relationship goes from A to B but not necessarily in the reverse direction.
     - **Example**: A **Twitter follow** relationship: If person A follows person B, the relationship is directed from A to B.

- o **Undirected Graph**: In an undirected graph, the edges do not have direction, meaning if there is an edge between nodes A and B, you can traverse it in both directions.
  - **Example**: A **friendship** in social networks, where if person A is friends with person B, person B is also friends with person A.

2. **Weighted vs. Unweighted Graphs**:
   - o **Weighted Graph**: In a weighted graph, each edge has a **weight** (or cost), representing the strength or cost of the connection. This is useful in applications like routing, where you need to consider the distance or cost between two points.
     - **Example**: A **road network** where the weight of an edge represents the **distance** between two cities.
   - o **Unweighted Graph**: In an unweighted graph, all edges are equal, meaning there is no cost or weight associated with traversing any edge.
     - **Example**: A **social network** where the edges simply represent connections between users (no weight).

Real-World Examples: Social Networks, Transport Networks

1. **Social Networks**:

○ **Graph Representation**: In a social network, individuals (or users) are represented as **nodes**, and their relationships (such as friendships or followers) are represented as **edges**. These relationships can be **directed** (such as a **follower relationship** on Twitter) or **undirected** (such as a **friendship** on Facebook).

○ **Example**: A social media platform like Facebook can be modeled as an undirected graph, where each user is a node, and friendships are undirected edges. On Twitter, the relationship is modeled as a directed graph, where one user can follow another user (but the relationship is not necessarily mutual).

2. **Transport Networks**:

○ **Graph Representation**: Transport networks (such as **railway systems**, **airlines**, or **roads**) can be represented using graphs where **stations** or **cities** are the nodes, and the **routes** between them (such as train tracks or flight paths) are the edges.

○ **Weighted Graph Example**: In a **road network**, each edge might be weighted by the **distance** or **travel time** between two cities, and the goal could be to find the **shortest path** (or least cost) from one city to another.

o **Undirected Graph Example**: In a **railway system**, the tracks might be undirected if trains can travel in both directions on the same track.

Representation: Adjacency Matrix vs. Adjacency List

To represent a graph in a computer, we need an efficient way to store the nodes and edges. There are two common ways to represent a graph: **adjacency matrix** and **adjacency list**.

1. **Adjacency Matrix**:
    o An **adjacency matrix** is a 2D array (matrix) used to represent a graph. The element at position (i, j) in the matrix represents the presence or absence of an edge between node i and node j.
    o **For undirected graphs**, the matrix is symmetric, meaning that if there is an edge between node i and node j, both matrix positions (i, j) and (j, i) are populated.
    o **For directed graphs**, the matrix is not necessarily symmetric, since an edge from node i to node j does not imply an edge from j to i.
    o **For weighted graphs**, the matrix elements store the weight of the edge instead of just 0 or 1.

Example of an Adjacency Matrix (Unweighted, Directed):

```
text
Copy
   0  1  2  3
0 [0, 1, 0, 0]
1 [0, 0, 1, 0]
2 [0, 0, 0, 1]
3 [0, 0, 0, 0]
```

In this matrix:

- There is an edge from node 0 to node 1.
- There is an edge from node 1 to node 2.
- There is an edge from node 2 to node 3.

Advantages:

- Easy to check if there is an edge between two nodes (O(1) time).

Disadvantages:

- Space inefficient for sparse graphs (lots of unused cells in the matrix).
- Difficult to store weighted edges.

2. **Adjacency List**:
   - An **adjacency list** is a collection of lists or arrays where each node has a list of adjacent nodes (its neighbors). For **directed graphs**, each node has a list of nodes it points to, and for **undirected**

104

graphs, each node has a list of nodes it is connected to.

Example of an Adjacency List (Unweighted, Directed):

```text
Copy
0 -> [1]
1 -> [2]
2 -> [3]
3 -> []
```

In this example:

- o Node 0 points to node 1.
- o Node 1 points to node 2.
- o Node 2 points to node 3.

Advantages:

- o Space efficient, especially for sparse graphs.
- o Efficient for iterating over the neighbors of a node.

Disadvantages:

105

○ Checking for the presence of an edge between two nodes can be slower than with an adjacency matrix (O(n) time in the worst case).

Depth-First Search (DFS) and Breadth-First Search (BFS) Algorithms

Graph traversal is the process of visiting all the nodes in a graph. There are two common ways to traverse a graph: **depth-first search (DFS)** and **breadth-first search (BFS)**. These algorithms are used to explore the nodes and edges of a graph, and they have a variety of applications such as **pathfinding**, **cycle detection**, and **network analysis**.

1. **Depth-First Search (DFS)**:
   ○ **DFS** explores a graph by going as deep as possible along a branch before backtracking. It starts at a node and explores each unvisited neighbor, diving deeper until it can no longer go further, at which point it backtracks to explore other paths.
   ○ **DFS Algorithm**:
      1. Start at the root node.
      2. Visit the first unvisited neighbor and continue down the path.

3. If no unvisited neighbors are left, backtrack and visit the next unvisited neighbor.

4. Repeat until all nodes have been visited.

o **DFS Example** (on the following graph):

```
text
Copy
      A
     / \
    B   C
   /     \
  D       E
```

DFS from node A:

- Visit A → B → D → backtrack → C → E.
- **Traversal order**: A, B, D, C, E.

DFS is useful for tasks like **cycle detection** and **finding connected components** in a graph.

2. **Breadth-First Search (BFS)**:
   o **BFS** explores a graph by visiting all of the neighbors at the present depth level before moving on to the nodes at the next depth level. It

starts at the root node and explores all of its neighbors before moving on to their neighbors.

- o **BFS Algorithm**:
    0. Start at the root node.
    1. Visit all unvisited neighbors at the current level.
    2. Move to the next level and repeat until all nodes are visited.
- o **BFS Example** (on the following graph):

```
text
Copy
      A
     / \
    B   C
   /     \
  D       E
```

BFS from node A:

- ▪ Visit A → B, C → D, E.
- ▪ **Traversal order**: A, B, C, D, E.

BFS is useful for tasks like **shortest pathfinding** in unweighted graphs.

Summary of Key Points:

- **Graphs** represent connections between entities and can be **directed** or **undirected**, and **weighted** or **unweighted**.
- **Adjacency matrices** and **adjacency lists** are common ways to represent graphs, with adjacency lists being more space-efficient for sparse graphs.
- **Real-world examples** include social networks and transport networks, where graphs are used to represent relationships and connections.
- **DFS and BFS** are two common algorithms used for **graph traversal**, with DFS exploring as deep as possible and BFS exploring level by level.
- **Heuristic applications** like job scheduling and pathfinding often rely on graph traversal to efficiently manage data and find solutions.

CHAPTER 11

SEARCHING ALGORITHMS – FINDING THE NEEDLE IN THE HAYSTACK

Linear Search, Binary Search Explained

Searching is a fundamental operation in computer science, used to find a specific element within a collection of data. Two of the most common searching algorithms are **linear search** and **binary search**, each with its strengths and weaknesses. These algorithms are essential tools for locating elements efficiently, but the method you choose depends on the type of data and the problem you're solving.

1. **Linear Search**:
   - **Definition**: A **linear search** is the simplest search algorithm. It works by checking each element of a collection (like an array or list) one at a time, starting from the first element and moving sequentially through the entire collection until the target element is found or all elements have been checked.
   - **How it works**:
     - Start from the first element.

- Compare the target element with the current element.
- If they match, return the index of the element.
- If not, move to the next element.
- Repeat until the element is found or the end of the list is reached.

Example: Searching for 7 in the list [5, 8, 3, 7, 9]:

```
text
Copy
Start at index 0: 5 != 7
Move to index 1: 8 != 7
Move to index 2: 3 != 7
Move to index 3: 7 == 7 (found it!)
```

o **Time Complexity: O(n)**, where n is the number of elements in the collection. In the worst case, you may have to check every element.

2. **Binary Search**:
   o **Definition**: **Binary search** is a much more efficient search algorithm, but it only works on **sorted** data. It repeatedly divides the search interval in half. If the value of the target is less than the value of the middle element, the search continues in the left half; otherwise, it continues in the right half.

111

- o **How it works**:
  - Start with the entire array (or list).
  - Find the middle element.
  - If the middle element is the target, return its index.
  - If the target is smaller than the middle element, repeat the search on the left half.
  - If the target is larger, repeat the search on the right half.
  - Repeat until the target is found or the search interval is empty.

Example: Searching for 7 in the sorted list [3, 5, 7, 8, 9]:

```
text
Copy
Middle element: 7 (found it!)
```

- o **Time Complexity: O(log n)**, where n is the number of elements in the list. Binary search significantly reduces the number of elements to check compared to linear search.

Real-World Examples: Searching in Databases and File Systems

1. **Searching in Databases**:

o Databases store vast amounts of data, and the ability to quickly search for information is crucial for performance. **Binary search** is commonly used in database indexing (e.g., B-trees, which are a balanced tree structure) to quickly find records.

o In a **relational database**, a query like SELECT * FROM users WHERE id = 7 uses a **searching algorithm** to find the record with the ID of 7. If the records are stored in a sorted order (or an index is maintained), binary search can be applied to make this lookup efficient.

o **Example**: Searching for a user by ID in a database. If the IDs are sorted, binary search can quickly locate the user without scanning the entire database.

2. **Searching in File Systems**:

o File systems are another area where searching algorithms are critical. When you search for a file in a directory, the file system must determine whether the file exists and, if so, return its location.

o **Linear search** may be used for searching in unsorted directories, but **binary search** is used if the directories or files are stored in a sorted order (e.g., alphabetical or by creation date).

113

- o **Example**: Searching for a specific file in a **sorted directory** on your computer. The file system can use **binary search** to find the file name quickly.

Time Complexity Comparison

The time complexity of a search algorithm indicates how the search time increases as the size of the data grows. Let's compare the time complexity of **linear search** and **binary search**:

- **Linear Search**:
  - o **Best case**: **O(1)** – The element is found on the first try.
  - o **Worst case**: **O(n)** – The element is at the end or not in the list at all, requiring a full traversal.
  - o **Average case**: **O(n)** – On average, half of the elements need to be checked.
- **Binary Search**:
  - o **Best case**: **O(1)** – The middle element is the target.
  - o **Worst case**: **O(log n)** – The search interval halves with each step, resulting in logarithmic growth.
  - o **Average case**: **O(log n)** – In general, binary search reduces the search space exponentially, making it much faster than linear search for large datasets.

114

In summary, **binary search** is far more efficient than **linear search** for large datasets, but it requires that the data be sorted. For **unsorted data**, **linear search** is the only option, but its performance can degrade significantly as the dataset grows.

Advanced Search Algorithms: Ternary Search and Interpolation Search

While **linear search** and **binary search** are widely known, there are other more specialized search algorithms that can be useful in certain situations.

1. **Ternary Search**:
   - **Ternary search** is a divide-and-conquer search algorithm, similar to binary search, but instead of dividing the array into two parts, it divides it into three. The algorithm compares the target with two middle elements and eliminates two-thirds of the search space at each step.
   - **When to use**: Ternary search is most effective when the array is **sorted**, and the function being searched is **unimodal** (i.e., increases and then decreases or decreases and then increases).
   - **Time Complexity**: $O(\log_3 n)$, which is similar to binary search, but may require more comparisons per step.

115

Example: Ternary search can be applied when searching for the maximum or minimum value in a unimodal function, such as in optimization problems.

2. **Interpolation Search**:

   o **Interpolation search** is an algorithm that works like **binary search**, but instead of dividing the search space in half, it tries to predict where the target value might be based on the values of the array. It works best when the data is uniformly distributed.

   o **How it works**: The algorithm calculates the "probe position" using a formula based on the value of the target and the values at the low and high ends of the range. It then compares the target to the element at that position and adjusts the range accordingly.

   o **When to use**: This algorithm is particularly useful when searching in a **uniformly distributed dataset**, where values are evenly spread out (e.g., searching for a particular number in a large range of numbers).

   o **Time Complexity**: In the best case (uniformly distributed data), **O(log log n)**, which is faster than binary search. However, in the worst case, it can degrade to **O(n)**, especially for non-uniformly distributed data.

Example: If you're searching for a **phone number** in a large, sorted **telephone directory** and you know that the numbers are evenly distributed, interpolation search can be more efficient than binary search.

Summary of Key Points:

- **Linear search** is simple but inefficient, with a time complexity of **O(n)** in the worst case.
- **Binary search** is much more efficient with a time complexity of **O(log n)** but requires sorted data.
- **Real-world examples** include searching in databases and file systems, where efficient searching algorithms are essential for performance.
- **Ternary search** divides the search space into three parts and is used for **unimodal data**.
- **Interpolation search** is used for uniformly distributed data and can achieve **O(log log n)** time complexity in the best case.

By understanding these searching algorithms and when to use them, you can select the most appropriate algorithm for your data and optimize performance in various applications.

CHAPTER 12

SORTING ALGORITHMS – ORGANIZING DATA EFFICIENTLY

Bubble Sort, Insertion Sort, Selection Sort, Quicksort, Mergesort

Sorting is one of the most fundamental tasks in computer science, where we organize data in a particular order (ascending or descending). Various sorting algorithms have been developed, each with different strengths and weaknesses. Let's explore five commonly used sorting algorithms: **Bubble Sort**, **Insertion Sort**, **Selection Sort**, **Quicksort**, and **Mergesort**.

1. **Bubble Sort**:
   o **Description**: **Bubble sort** works by repeatedly swapping adjacent elements that are in the wrong order. The process is repeated for each element in the array until the array is sorted. The algorithm "bubbles" the largest unsorted element to its correct position in each pass through the list.
   o **How it works**:
      ▪ Compare adjacent elements.
      ▪ If the first element is greater than the second, swap them.

- Repeat this for all elements in the list, iterating multiple times until no swaps are needed.

Example: Sorting the list [5, 2, 9, 1] using bubble sort:

```
text
Copy
Pass 1: [2, 5, 1, 9]
Pass 2: [2, 1, 5, 9]
Pass 3: [1, 2, 5, 9] (sorted)
```

- o **Time Complexity: O(n²)**, where n is the number of elements in the list. In the worst case, each element is compared with every other element.
- o **Space Complexity: O(1)** – Bubble sort is an in-place sorting algorithm, meaning it uses a constant amount of extra space.

Use Case: Best for small datasets or when simplicity is a priority.

2. **Insertion Sort**:
   - o **Description: Insertion sort** builds the sorted array one element at a time. It assumes the first element is sorted and then repeatedly inserts the

next element into its correct position among the already sorted elements.

- o **How it works**:
  - Start with the second element and compare it to the first.
  - If it's smaller, move the first element to the right and insert the second element in the first position.
  - Continue inserting elements one by one until the list is sorted.

Example: Sorting the list [5, 2, 9, 1] using insertion sort:

```
text
Copy
Pass 1: [2, 5, 9, 1]
Pass 2: [2, 5, 9, 1]
Pass 3: [1, 2, 5, 9] (sorted)
```

- o **Time Complexity**: **O(n²)** in the worst case, but **O(n)** in the best case when the data is already nearly sorted.
- o **Space Complexity**: **O(1)** – Like bubble sort, insertion sort is an in-place sorting algorithm.

Use Case: Suitable for small datasets or nearly sorted data. It's also efficient for online sorting (sorting a list that is constantly growing).

3. **Selection Sort**:
   o **Description**: **Selection sort** works by repeatedly finding the smallest (or largest) element from the unsorted part of the array and swapping it with the first unsorted element.
   o **How it works**:
      - Find the minimum element in the unsorted part of the array.
      - Swap it with the first unsorted element.
      - Repeat until the entire array is sorted.

Example: Sorting the list [5, 2, 9, 1] using selection sort:

```
text
Copy
Pass 1: [1, 2, 9, 5]
Pass 2: [1, 2, 9, 5]
Pass 3: [1, 2, 5, 9] (sorted)
```

   o **Time Complexity**: **O(n²)**, as the algorithm always needs to check all remaining elements to find the minimum.

121

- o **Space Complexity**: **O(1)** – Selection sort is also an in-place sorting algorithm.

Use Case: Good for small datasets where memory space is limited and simplicity is desired.

4. **Quicksort**:
    - o **Description**: **Quicksort** is a divide-and-conquer algorithm that selects a **pivot** element and partitions the array into two subarrays: one with elements smaller than the pivot and one with elements larger. The subarrays are then sorted recursively.
    - o **How it works**:
        - Select a pivot element.
        - Partition the array into two subarrays: one with elements smaller than the pivot and one with elements larger.
        - Recursively apply quicksort to both subarrays.
        - Combine the subarrays into a sorted array.

Example: Sorting the list [5, 2, 9, 1] using quicksort (choosing pivot as the last element):

```
text
Copy
```

```
Pivot: 1
Partition: [1, 2, 9, 5]
Recursively sort [2, 5, 9] and [1]
```

- o **Time Complexity**: **O(n log n)** on average, but **O(n²)** in the worst case (if the pivot is always the smallest or largest element).
- o **Space Complexity**: **O(log n)** for the recursive stack.

Use Case: Quicksort is one of the most efficient algorithms for large datasets and is often used in practice for general-purpose sorting.

5. **Mergesort**:
- o **Description**: **Mergesort** is another divide-and-conquer algorithm. It divides the array into two halves, recursively sorts each half, and then merges the two sorted halves into a single sorted array.
- o **How it works**:
  - Split the array into two halves.
  - Recursively sort each half.
  - Merge the sorted halves back together.

Example: Sorting the list [5, 2, 9, 1] using mergesort:

123

```
text
Copy
Split: [5, 2] and [9, 1]
Recursively sort: [2, 5] and [1, 9]
Merge: [1, 2, 5, 9]
```

- o **Time Complexity**: **O(n log n)** for both average and worst cases.
- o **Space Complexity**: **O(n)** due to the space required for merging.

Use Case: Mergesort is ideal for **external sorting** where large amounts of data are sorted that do not fit in memory, as it works efficiently with large data sets.

Time Complexity and Space Complexity of Sorting Algorithms

Here's a comparison of the time and space complexities of the sorting algorithms we discussed:

Algorithm	Time Complexity (Best)	Time Complexity (Average)	Time Complexity (Worst)	Space Complexity
Bubble Sort	O(n)	O(n²)	O(n²)	O(1)

Algorithm	Time Complexity (Best)	Time Complexity (Average)	Time Complexity (Worst)	Space Complexity
Insertion Sort	O(n)	O(n²)	O(n²)	O(1)
Selection Sort	O(n²)	O(n²)	O(n²)	O(1)
Quicksort	O(n log n)	O(n log n)	O(n²)	O(log n)
Mergesort	O(n log n)	O(n log n)	O(n log n)	O(n)

- **Time Complexity**: Indicates how the runtime of the algorithm increases as the size of the dataset increases.
- **Space Complexity**: Indicates how much extra memory the algorithm needs in addition to the input data.

Use Cases for Each Sorting Algorithm

1. **Bubble Sort**:
   - **Use case**: Bubble sort is rarely used in practice due to its inefficiency, but it is suitable for educational purposes and small datasets where simplicity is more important than performance.
   - **Example**: Sorting small datasets where ease of implementation is key.

125

2. **Insertion Sort**:

   o **Use case**: Best suited for **small datasets** or data that is already partially sorted. It performs well with **real-time applications** where new data is inserted one element at a time (e.g., inserting records in an ordered list).

   o **Example**: Sorting a nearly sorted list or when data arrives incrementally (e.g., insertion into a database).

3. **Selection Sort**:

   o **Use case**: Similar to bubble sort, it is rarely used for large datasets. Selection sort is simple and easy to implement, making it useful for scenarios where memory usage is a constraint and the data set is small.

   o **Example**: Sorting small datasets with minimal memory requirements.

4. **Quicksort**:

   o **Use case**: One of the most efficient algorithms for **general-purpose sorting**, widely used in practice for large datasets. It is especially efficient for sorting data stored in memory.

   o **Example**: Sorting large datasets in systems where performance is critical (e.g., database sorting).

5. **Mergesort**:

- o **Use case**: Mergesort is ideal for **external sorting** (where the data is too large to fit in memory), as it works well with linked lists and large data sets. It's also stable, meaning it preserves the order of equal elements.
- o **Example**: Sorting large data sets stored on disk or external memory.

Summary of Key Points:

- **Sorting algorithms** are essential for organizing data efficiently, with each algorithm having its own strengths and weaknesses.
- **Bubble Sort**, **Insertion Sort**, and **Selection Sort** are simple but inefficient, with $O(n^2)$ time complexity in the worst case.
- **Quicksort** and **Mergesort** are more efficient algorithms with $O(n \log n)$ time complexity, making them suitable for large datasets.
- **Space complexity** is an important consideration, with algorithms like **Mergesort** requiring additional memory, while others like **Quicksort** and **Selection Sort** operate in-place.

Understanding these algorithms and their trade-offs allows you to choose the most appropriate one depending on the size of the dataset, the environment (e.g., in-memory vs. external data), and the need for stability or efficiency.

CHAPTER 13

DIVIDE AND CONQUER – BREAKING DOWN PROBLEMS

Introduction to Divide and Conquer Approach

The **divide and conquer** (D&C) strategy is a powerful approach for solving problems that can be broken down into smaller, more manageable sub-problems. It's a fundamental algorithmic technique used in computer science and software development. The core idea behind divide and conquer is:

1. **Divide**: Break the problem into smaller, simpler sub-problems.
2. **Conquer**: Solve each sub-problem independently, typically recursively.
3. **Combine**: Merge the solutions to the sub-problems to form the solution to the original problem.

This technique is especially useful for **recursive problems**, where the solution to a problem can be obtained by solving smaller instances of the same problem.

Real-World Examples: Merge Sort, Quicksort

Two of the most famous algorithms that implement the divide and conquer strategy are **Merge Sort** and **Quicksort**. Both algorithms break down the problem into smaller sub-problems and solve them independently before combining the results.

1. **Merge Sort**:
   - **Merge sort** is a classic example of a divide and conquer algorithm. The array is divided into two halves, each half is sorted recursively, and then the two sorted halves are merged back together into a single sorted array.
   - **How it works**:
     1. Divide the array into two halves.
     2. Recursively sort each half.
     3. Merge the two sorted halves to get a sorted array.

   Example:

   - Input: [5, 2, 9, 1]
   - Divide: [5, 2] and [9, 1]
   - Recursively sort: [2, 5] and [1, 9]
   - Merge: [1, 2, 5, 9]

Time Complexity: **O(n log n)**, where n is the number of elements in the array. **Space Complexity**: **O(n)**, due to the additional space required for merging the two halves.

2. **Quicksort**:
   - **Quicksort** is another divide and conquer algorithm that works by selecting a **pivot** element, partitioning the array into two sub-arrays (elements smaller than the pivot and elements larger than the pivot), and then recursively sorting the sub-arrays.
   - **How it works**:
     1. Choose a pivot element.
     2. Partition the array into two sub-arrays: one with elements less than the pivot, and the other with elements greater than the pivot.
     3. Recursively apply quicksort to the sub-arrays.
     4. Combine the results (since each sub-array is sorted, no additional merging is required).

Example:

   - Input: [5, 2, 9, 1]
   - Pivot: 1

o Partition: `[1], [2, 5, 9]`

o Recursively sort the second sub-array: `[2, 5, 9]`

o Final sorted array: `[1, 2, 5, 9]`

Time Complexity: **O(n log n)** on average, but **O(n²)** in the worst case (if the pivot is always the smallest or largest element). **Space Complexity**: **O(log n)** for the recursive stack.

How Problems Can Be Divided into Smaller Sub-Problems

In a divide and conquer approach, the key to success lies in identifying how a large problem can be broken down into smaller, manageable sub-problems. Here's how you can think about dividing problems into sub-problems:

1. **Recursive Structure**:

   o Many problems exhibit a **recursive structure**, meaning that the solution to the problem involves solving smaller instances of the same problem. For instance, in sorting algorithms like **merge sort** and **quicksort**, the problem of sorting an entire array is reduced to the problem of sorting smaller sub-arrays, which are easier to solve.

Example: Sorting a large list is divided into sorting two smaller sub-lists, each of which can be further divided.

132

2. **Sub-Problem Independence**:

    o   The sub-problems should be **independent** of each other, meaning they can be solved separately without affecting each other. This allows parallel processing, which can significantly speed up the solution.

    Example: In **merge sort**, the two halves of the array are sorted independently before they are merged, making the two sub-problems independent.

3. **Combination of Solutions**:

    o   After solving the sub-problems, the next step is to **combine** the solutions to get the overall solution. The combination step can be simple or complex, depending on the problem.

    Example: In **merge sort**, the combination step is merging two sorted arrays into one sorted array.

Key Strategies and Applications in Real-World Software Development

The divide and conquer strategy is widely used in real-world software development, especially when working with large datasets, recursive problems, and performance optimization. Here are some key strategies and applications:

1. **Sorting**:

    o Sorting algorithms like **quicksort**, **mergesort**, and **heap sort** use the divide and conquer approach to efficiently sort large datasets.

    Example: In e-commerce applications, sorting is essential for displaying product lists based on criteria like price, popularity, or rating. These sorting algorithms are highly efficient and allow the application to handle large inventories.

2. **Searching**:

    o Searching algorithms like **binary search** and **ternary search** also use divide and conquer strategies to efficiently search through sorted datasets.

    Example: **Binary search** is used in databases for quickly finding a record. **Interpolation search** can be used in applications where data is uniformly distributed, like looking for specific data points in scientific computations.

3. **Graph Algorithms**:

    o Many **graph algorithms** like **depth-first search (DFS)** and **breadth-first search (BFS)** can be considered divide and conquer, as they break the graph into smaller parts (subgraphs or nodes) and explore each part recursively.

Example: In social media applications, graphs are used to represent user connections, and algorithms like DFS or BFS are used to find relationships or clusters in the network.

4. **Dynamic Programming (Memoization)**:
   o Divide and conquer is often combined with **dynamic programming** (DP) to solve problems by breaking them into overlapping sub-problems and storing intermediate results to avoid redundant computations.

Example: **Fibonacci sequence** computation, where each number depends on the previous two, is efficiently solved using DP by storing previously computed values.

5. **Parallel Processing**:
   o Since divide and conquer algorithms often solve sub-problems independently, they are ideal candidates for **parallel processing**. Sub-problems can be processed simultaneously on different processors, drastically reducing execution time for large datasets.

135

Example: In **distributed systems**, divide and conquer algorithms like **map-reduce** are used for processing large datasets across multiple machines or nodes.

6. **Divide and Conquer in Computational Geometry**:
   o In **computational geometry**, problems like finding the **closest pair of points, convex hull**, or **line segment intersection** often use divide and conquer to efficiently solve the problem in less time than brute force methods.

Example: Finding the **closest pair of points** in a 2D space using divide and conquer.

7. **Divide and Conquer in Machine Learning**:
   o In **machine learning**, divide and conquer strategies can be applied to problems like decision tree construction, random forest algorithms, and support vector machines, where datasets are split into smaller parts and then combined for predictions or classification tasks.

Example: **Random forests** use the divide and conquer approach to create multiple decision trees from different subsets of the data and then combine the results to make more accurate predictions.

Summary of Key Points:

- The **divide and conquer** approach breaks a problem into smaller sub-problems, solves them independently, and then combines the results.
- **Real-world examples** include sorting algorithms (e.g., **merge sort** and **quicksort**) and searching algorithms (e.g., **binary search**).
- Divide and conquer is widely used in **software development**, especially in areas like sorting, searching, graph algorithms, and machine learning.
- **Key strategies** in D&C involve recursion, independence of sub-problems, and efficient combination of solutions.
- The technique enables **parallel processing**, **dynamic programming**, and more efficient algorithms, making it indispensable in performance-critical applications.

CHAPTER 14

DYNAMIC PROGRAMMING – SOLVING PROBLEMS OPTIMALLY

What is Dynamic Programming (DP)?

Dynamic Programming (DP) is a method for solving complex problems by breaking them down into simpler subproblems. It is used when the problem has the following two key properties:

1. **Optimal Substructure**: This means that the optimal solution to the problem can be constructed efficiently from optimal solutions to its subproblems.
2. **Overlapping Subproblems**: This means that the problem can be broken down into subproblems that are solved multiple times, making it inefficient to solve them repeatedly.

The central idea of DP is to **store** the solutions to subproblems to avoid redundant calculations. This is done using either **memoization** (top-down approach) or **tabulation** (bottom-up approach), making it an efficient way to solve problems that involve overlapping subproblems.

138

DP is commonly used in **optimization problems**, where you need to find the best solution among a large set of possible solutions.

Real-World Example: Optimal Substructure and Overlapping Subproblems

1. **Optimal Substructure**:
   - A problem has **optimal substructure** if the solution to the problem can be constructed from the solutions to its subproblems. This property is key in dynamic programming.
   - **Example**: In the **Fibonacci sequence**, the value of **Fib(n)** is defined as the sum of **Fib(n-1)** and **Fib(n-2)**. So, if we know the solutions to the subproblems **Fib(n-1)** and **Fib(n-2)**, we can compute **Fib(n)**.
2. **Overlapping Subproblems**:
   - A problem has **overlapping subproblems** if it can be broken down into subproblems that are solved multiple times. Instead of solving the same subproblems repeatedly, DP stores the results of subproblems and reuses them.
   - **Example**: In the **knapsack problem**, subproblems involving smaller capacities or items are solved multiple times in different branches of the recursion. DP avoids

139

recomputing these subproblems by storing their solutions.

DP Solutions to Problems Like Fibonacci, Knapsack, Longest Common Subsequence

1. **Fibonacci Sequence**:
   o **Problem**: The Fibonacci sequence is defined by the recurrence relation:

   $Fib(n)=Fib(n-1)+Fib(n-2)Fib(n) = Fib(n-1) + Fib(n-2)Fib(n)=Fib(n-1)+Fib(n-2)$

   with base cases **Fib(0) = 0** and **Fib(1) = 1**.

   o **Solution with DP**: A naive recursive approach would recompute the same Fibonacci numbers multiple times, leading to exponential time complexity. Using dynamic programming, we store the results of previously computed Fibonacci numbers to avoid redundant calculations.

   Bottom-up Approach (Tabulation):

```python
Copy
def fibonacci(n):
```

```
dp = [0] * (n + 1)
dp[1] = 1
for i in range(2, n + 1):
    dp[i] = dp[i-1] + dp[i-2]
return dp[n]
```

- o **Time Complexity**: **O(n)** – We only compute each Fibonacci number once.
- o **Space Complexity**: **O(n)** – We store the results of all subproblems.

2. **Knapsack Problem**:

- o **Problem**: You are given a set of items, each with a weight and a value, and a knapsack that can hold a limited weight. The goal is to maximize the total value of items that can fit into the knapsack without exceeding its weight capacity.

- o **Solution with DP**: This is a classic example of an optimization problem. We can use dynamic programming to solve it by storing the results of subproblems, where each subproblem involves a subset of items and a certain weight capacity.

Bottom-up Approach (Tabulation):

```python
Copy
def knapsack(weights, values, capacity):
    n = len(weights)
```

141

```
dp = [[0] * (capacity + 1) for _ in
range(n + 1)]
    for i in range(1, n + 1):
        for w in range(1, capacity + 1):
            if weights[i-1] <= w:
                dp[i][w] = max(dp[i-1][w],
dp[i-1][w-weights[i-1]] + values[i-1])
            else:
                dp[i][w] = dp[i-1][w]
    return dp[n][capacity]
```

- o **Time Complexity**: **O(n * W)** – n is the number of items, and W is the weight capacity of the knapsack.
- o **Space Complexity**: **O(n * W)** – We store a table of size n * W for memoization.

3. **Longest Common Subsequence (LCS)**:
   - o **Problem**: Given two sequences, find the longest subsequence that appears in both sequences.
   - o **Solution with DP**: LCS is a well-known problem in dynamic programming. We build a table where each entry dp[i][j] stores the length of the longest common subsequence of the first i characters of one string and the first j characters of the other string.

Bottom-up Approach (Tabulation):

142

```python
Copy
def lcs(X, Y):
    m, n = len(X), len(Y)
    dp = [[0] * (n + 1) for _ in range(m +
1)]
    for i in range(1, m + 1):
        for j in range(1, n + 1):
            if X[i-1] == Y[j-1]:
                dp[i][j] = dp[i-1][j-1] +
1
            else:
                dp[i][j] = max(dp[i-1][j],
dp[i][j-1])
    return dp[m][n]
```

- o **Time Complexity**: **O(m * n)** – Where m and n are the lengths of the two strings.
- o **Space Complexity**: **O(m * n)** – The table requires m * n space.

Top-down vs. Bottom-up Approach

1. **Top-down Approach (Memoization)**:
   - o The top-down approach uses **recursion** and stores the results of subproblems as they are computed to avoid redundant calculations. This technique is known as **memoization**.

143

- o In the top-down approach, you solve the problem recursively and, whenever a subproblem is solved, store the result in a **cache** (typically a dictionary or array).

- o **Example**: Fibonacci sequence using memoization:

```python
Copy
def fibonacci_top_down(n, memo={}):
    if n <= 1:
        return n
    if n not in memo:
        memo[n] = fibonacci_top_down(n-1,
memo) + fibonacci_top_down(n-2, memo)
    return memo[n]
```

- o **Advantages**: Easy to implement and intuitive when converting a recursive solution into a DP solution.

- o **Disadvantages**: Requires extra memory for storing results, and there is some overhead due to recursion.

2. **Bottom-up Approach (Tabulation)**:

- o The bottom-up approach solves the problem iteratively, starting with the smallest subproblems and gradually building up the solution to the original problem.

144

o This approach involves filling a table (often a 2D array or a 1D array) with the solutions to all subproblems and then using these solutions to build the final result.

o **Example**: Fibonacci sequence using tabulation:

```python
Copy
def fibonacci_bottom_up(n):
    dp = [0] * (n + 1)
    dp[1] = 1
    for i in range(2, n + 1):
        dp[i] = dp[i-1] + dp[i-2]
    return dp[n]
```

o **Advantages**: Typically more efficient than the top-down approach, especially for problems with overlapping subproblems. It avoids recursion overhead.

o **Disadvantages**: Less intuitive for problems that are naturally recursive.

Summary of Key Points:

- **Dynamic programming (DP)** is a powerful technique used to solve problems with **optimal substructure** and **overlapping subproblems** by breaking the problem into smaller subproblems and storing the results to avoid redundant calculations.

- **Real-world examples** of DP include problems like the **Fibonacci sequence**, the **knapsack problem**, and the **longest common subsequence**.
- **Top-down (memoization)** and **bottom-up (tabulation)** are two different approaches to solving DP problems, each with its own strengths and weaknesses.
- The **bottom-up approach** is often more efficient because it avoids recursion overhead and directly solves the problem iteratively, but the **top-down approach** is more intuitive for problems with recursive structures.

CHAPTER 15

GREEDY ALGORITHMS – TAKING THE BEST IMMEDIATE CHOICE

Greedy Method Explained with Examples

A **greedy algorithm** is a simple, intuitive approach to solving optimization problems by making the **best choice at each step** with the hope that these local choices will lead to a globally optimal solution. The key idea is to **always pick the best option available** at the moment without worrying about future consequences.

The **greedy method** works by solving a problem in stages, where each stage involves choosing the best option available without reconsidering previous choices. Greedy algorithms are often used for problems where local optimality leads to global optimality.

1. **How Greedy Algorithms Work**:
   - The algorithm starts with an empty solution.
   - In each step, it chooses the **best option** (the local optimum) available.
   - It adds this choice to the solution and moves to the next step.

○ The algorithm doesn't backtrack or reconsider previous choices, which is a key characteristic of greedy algorithms.

Example: Consider a **fractional knapsack problem**, where you are given items with weights and values, and you have a knapsack with a limited capacity. The greedy approach is to take items in order of the highest **value-to-weight ratio** and fill the knapsack until it's full. The goal is to maximize the total value in the knapsack by making the best local choice at each step.

Real-World Examples: Activity Selection Problem, Coin Change Problem

1. **Activity Selection Problem**:
   ○ **Problem**: You are given a set of activities, each with a start time and an end time, and you need to select the maximum number of activities that can be performed by a single person, assuming no overlap between selected activities.
   ○ **Greedy Approach**: The greedy solution is to always choose the activity that finishes **earliest** (has the smallest end time), as this leaves the maximum remaining time for other activities.

Steps:

3.   Sort the activities by their end times.

4. Select the activity that finishes first.

5. Repeat the process for the remaining activities, but only select activities that start after the previously selected one finishes.

Example: Suppose you have the following activities with start and end times:

```
text
Copy
Activity 1: (1, 3)
Activity 2: (2, 5)
Activity 3: (4, 6)
Activity 4: (5, 7)
Activity 5: (8, 9)
```

The greedy approach selects the activities in the following order:

- ○ First, select **Activity 1** (ends at 3).
- ○ Then, select **Activity 3** (starts at 4, ends at 6).
- ○ Finally, select **Activity 5** (starts at 8, ends at 9).

The selected activities are **Activity 1**, **Activity 3**, and **Activity 5**.

2. **Coin Change Problem**:

o **Problem**: You are given a set of coin denominations and a target value. The goal is to find the minimum number of coins that make up the target value.

o **Greedy Approach**: The greedy solution is to start with the largest denomination and use as many of those coins as possible, then move to the next largest denomination, and continue until the target value is reached.

Example: Given the coin denominations [1, 5, 10, 25] and a target amount of **30**, the greedy approach would work as follows:

o Start with the largest coin (25), use one coin of 25.

o The remaining amount is 30 - 25 = 5.

o Use one coin of 5.

o The remaining amount is 0, so the total number of coins used is 2.

The greedy approach gives the solution: **2 coins** (1 of 25, 1 of 5).

Note: The greedy approach works for coin change problems when the denominations have certain properties, such as the **denominations being multiples of smaller denominations** (e.g., [1, 5, 10, 25]).

Key Features: Optimality and Local vs. Global Decision-Making

1. **Optimality**:
   - Greedy algorithms are **not guaranteed** to always provide the **optimal solution** for all problems. In some cases, they give a solution that is close to optimal, but in other cases, the solution may be suboptimal.
   - **Example**: The **coin change problem** can be solved optimally using a greedy algorithm if the coin denominations follow certain properties (such as being multiples of each other). However, for arbitrary coin denominations (e.g., [1, 3, 4] for a target of 6), the greedy approach might not yield the optimal solution.

2. **Local vs. Global Decision-Making**:
   - In a greedy algorithm, decisions are made based on **local information**—i.e., the best choice at each step, without considering future consequences.
   - **Local Decision-Making**: The algorithm picks the option that looks best in the current step (such as choosing the smallest end time in the activity

selection problem or the largest denomination in the coin change problem).

o **Global Decision-Making**: The algorithm hopes that these local choices will lead to a globally optimal solution, but this is not always the case.

Example: In the **activity selection problem**, the local decision of picking the activity that finishes earliest leads to the globally optimal solution of selecting the maximum number of non-overlapping activities. However, in some problems (such as the coin change problem with arbitrary denominations), this approach does not always result in the global optimal solution.

Time Complexity and Use Cases

1. **Time Complexity**:
   o The time complexity of a greedy algorithm depends on how the greedy decisions are made and whether sorting or searching is involved:
     ▪ For example, in the **activity selection problem**, sorting the activities by their end times takes **O(n log n)**, where n is the number of activities, and then the greedy choice (picking the activity with the earliest end time) is **O(n)**. Hence, the overall time complexity is **O(n log n)**.

- In the **coin change problem**, sorting the denominations takes **O(m log m)**, where m is the number of denominations, and the greedy algorithm runs in **O(n)**, where n is the target amount. Thus, the time complexity can be roughly **O(m log m + n)**.

2. **Use Cases**:

   o **Activity Selection Problem**: When you need to maximize the number of non-overlapping activities or events (e.g., scheduling tasks or events).

   o **Coin Change Problem**: When the coin denominations allow for efficient change-making (e.g., currency exchange, or vending machine design where the denominations are multiples of each other).

   o **Huffman Coding**: In data compression, greedy algorithms are used to generate the optimal prefix-free binary codes for characters.

   o **Minimum Spanning Tree**: Algorithms like **Kruskal's** and **Prim's** use a greedy approach to find the minimum spanning tree in a weighted graph.

o **Dijkstra's Shortest Path Algorithm**: Greedy approach is used to find the shortest path between nodes in a graph.

Summary of Key Points:

- **Greedy algorithms** work by making the best immediate choice at each step with the hope of finding the globally optimal solution.
- They are **optimal** for certain problems (e.g., **activity selection** and **coin change problem** with specific denominations) but may not always guarantee an optimal solution for all problems.
- **Local decisions** are made based on the best available option at each step, and these decisions are assumed to lead to a **globally optimal solution**.
- **Time complexity** is often **O(n log n)** due to sorting, and greedy algorithms are generally efficient and easy to implement.
- **Use cases** include problems like **activity selection, coin change, Huffman coding, minimum spanning trees**, and **shortest path finding**.

Greedy algorithms are an essential tool in optimization problems, but they must be used with caution, as they are not always guaranteed to provide the best solution for every problem. They

154

are ideal for scenarios where local optimal choices lead to the global optimum.

CHAPTER 16

BACKTRACKING – EXPLORING ALL POSSIBILITIES

What is Backtracking? When to Use It

Backtracking is a problem-solving algorithmic technique for finding **all possible solutions** to a problem by trying to build a solution step-by-step and abandoning (or **backtracking**) as soon as we determine that the current solution cannot be extended to a valid solution. It is essentially a way of **exploring all possible options** in a search space by following a trial-and-error approach.

Backtracking is used when:

1. The problem involves finding all possible solutions or just one solution that satisfies certain constraints.
2. The problem has **multiple constraints** that must be satisfied simultaneously.
3. The solution space is **large** and cannot be solved through simple iteration.

Backtracking works by:

- **Exploring the solution space** recursively.
- At each step, making a choice that seems appropriate.

- **Backtracking** when the choice doesn't lead to a solution (i.e., when it violates one of the constraints or results in an infeasible solution).

This method is especially useful for problems where brute-force exploration of all possibilities would be inefficient, but we can efficiently prune branches that are unlikely to lead to a valid solution.

Real-World Examples: Solving Mazes, N-Queens Problem

1. **Solving Mazes**:
   - **Problem**: Given a maze, find a path from the start to the end.
   - **Backtracking Approach**: The maze can be represented as a grid, where each cell has a state (either open or blocked). The backtracking algorithm starts at the entrance, recursively tries to move in possible directions (up, down, left, right), and backtracks when it hits a dead-end or an already visited cell.

Steps:

3. Start at the initial point.
4. Explore all possible moves (up, down, left, right).
5. If a move leads to a dead-end, backtrack and try another direction.

157

6. Continue until the destination is reached or all possible paths are explored.

Time Complexity: In the worst case, backtracking will explore all possible paths, leading to **O(2^n)** time complexity for some problems (depending on the maze size).

2. **N-Queens Problem**:
   o **Problem**: Place **n** queens on an **n x n** chessboard such that no two queens threaten each other. This means no two queens can share the same row, column, or diagonal.
   o **Backtracking Approach**: The algorithm starts by placing a queen in the first row and tries to place queens in subsequent rows. It backtracks when it finds that a queen cannot be placed without violating the constraints.

Steps:

2. Place a queen in the first row.
3. Try placing the next queen in the next row, ensuring that no two queens share a column or diagonal.

4. If a queen cannot be placed, backtrack to the previous row and try a new position for that queen.

5. Repeat until all queens are placed or all possibilities are exhausted.

Time Complexity: The time complexity of solving the N-Queens problem using backtracking is **O(n!)**, as there are n! ways to place queens on the board.

Key Strategies for Backtracking Algorithms

1. **Recursion**:
   o Backtracking typically involves recursion, where the function calls itself to try different possibilities at each level of the search tree.

2. **Pruning**:
   o **Pruning** refers to eliminating branches in the search tree that are guaranteed to lead to invalid solutions. This helps in reducing the search space and improving efficiency.
   o For example, if placing a queen on the current position violates a constraint (such as another queen in the same column or diagonal), we prune that branch and do not explore further along that path.

3. **Trial-and-Error**:

- o The algorithm proceeds by trying one possibility, and if that doesn't work, it backtracks to the previous decision point and tries the next possibility.

4. **Constraint Checking**:
   - o In every step of backtracking, we check whether the current partial solution satisfies all the constraints of the problem. If it doesn't, we discard that solution and backtrack.

5. **Stacking State**:
   - o The algorithm often maintains a state that represents the current configuration. Each recursive call represents a new state. When backtracking occurs, the state is "rolled back" to a previous valid state.

Optimization Techniques to Prune Search Trees

Backtracking can be inefficient if it explores all possible combinations without pruning invalid branches. There are several techniques to optimize backtracking and prune the search tree:

1. **Forward Checking**:
   - o In this technique, before making a move, we check the **future validity** of the current choice. If the choice is incompatible with future moves, we prune that branch early.

- o **Example**: In the **N-Queens problem**, before placing a queen in a column, we check whether placing the queen in the current row would conflict with future rows and diagonals.

2. **Constraint Propagation**:
   - o **Constraint propagation** involves adjusting the constraints dynamically as we make decisions. For example, in constraint satisfaction problems like Sudoku, placing a number in a cell can reduce the possible values for other cells. By propagating these changes forward, we can prune invalid choices early.

3. **Heuristics**:
   - o **Heuristic techniques** like **most constrained variable** (MCV) and **least-constraining value** (LCV) can help guide the search towards the most promising solutions first.
   - o **Example**: In the N-Queens problem, we could use the MCV heuristic to place queens in columns that are most likely to cause conflicts first, allowing for faster pruning.

4. **Memoization**:
   - o **Memoization** is used in some backtracking problems to avoid re-exploring the same state multiple times. Storing the results of previously

computed subproblems can significantly reduce redundant work.

5. **Branch and Bound**:
   - o This is an optimization technique often used with backtracking to further prune the search tree. It involves calculating a **bound** (an estimate of the best possible solution) and discarding branches where the best possible solution is worse than the current best solution.
   - o **Example**: In the **knapsack problem**, if the current partial solution's value is less than the best-known solution, the branch is pruned.

6. **Symmetry Breaking**:
   - o For problems with symmetries (e.g., the N-Queens problem, where swapping rows or columns results in the same solution), symmetry-breaking rules can be applied to reduce redundant solutions.

Example: In the N-Queens problem, if the solution is symmetric (i.e., swapping rows or columns yields the same solution), we can break the symmetry by considering only one half of the possible configurations.

Real-World Applications of Backtracking

Backtracking is widely used in problems that involve finding combinations, permutations, or paths, especially in optimization problems where we need to find the best solution out of a large number of possibilities. Here are some real-world applications of backtracking:

1. **Puzzle Solving**:
   o Backtracking is commonly used to solve puzzles such as **Sudoku, crossword puzzles**, and the **8-puzzle problem**, where the algorithm explores all possible configurations until a valid solution is found.

2. **Combinatorial Optimization**:
   o Problems like the **Traveling Salesman Problem (TSP), knapsack problem**, and **graph coloring** often use backtracking to find the best combination of decisions.

3. **Pathfinding**:
   o In games or simulations, backtracking is used to find a path in a maze or between points in a graph. It's used in AI algorithms for games, like **chess** or **maze-solving robots**.

4. **Constraint Satisfaction Problems (CSP)**:
   o Backtracking is used to solve constraint satisfaction problems such as **Sudoku, map**

163

coloring, and **job scheduling**, where you must satisfy multiple constraints while finding a solution.

5. **Decision Making and Scheduling**:

   o Backtracking is applied to solve scheduling problems like **job-shop scheduling**, where tasks need to be scheduled with constraints like time, resources, and dependencies.

Summary of Key Points:

- **Backtracking** is a powerful algorithmic technique used for exploring all possible solutions to a problem by building solutions incrementally and abandoning (backtracking) as soon as we realize that a particular solution cannot be extended to a valid one.

- **Real-world applications** of backtracking include solving puzzles (e.g., Sudoku), optimization problems (e.g., N-Queens, knapsack), and pathfinding problems (e.g., maze solving).

- **Key strategies** include recursion, pruning, constraint checking, and memoization, all of which improve the efficiency of backtracking algorithms.

- **Optimization techniques** such as forward checking, constraint propagation, and branch-and-bound can help to reduce the size of the search space and make backtracking algorithms more efficient.

CHAPTER 17

ADVANCED TREES – B-TREES AND TRIES

B-Trees: Usage in Databases for Indexing

B-Trees are a specialized type of self-balancing **search tree** that maintains sorted data and allows for efficient insertion, deletion, and search operations. They are specifically designed to **optimize disk storage** and **minimize disk access** by reducing the height of the tree and allowing nodes to store multiple values. This makes B-trees highly suitable for **databases** and **file systems** where large amounts of data need to be stored and accessed quickly.

1. **B-Tree Structure**:
   - A **B-tree** is a balanced tree where each node contains multiple keys and has multiple children. The tree ensures that the keys are sorted and that the tree is balanced, meaning all leaf nodes are at the same depth.
   - The number of children per node is constrained to a minimum and maximum, ensuring the tree remains balanced.
2. **Key Properties of B-Trees**:
   - **Balanced**: All leaf nodes are at the same depth.

166

- o **Sorted**: Keys are stored in a sorted order within each node.

- o **Multilevel Nodes**: Each node can have more than two children (unlike binary trees), which helps in reducing the height of the tree, improving search performance.

Example of a B-tree (order 3):

text
Copy

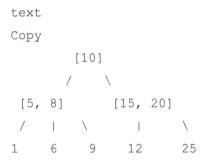

```
          [10]
          /    \
  [5, 8]          [15, 20]
  /  |  \          |    \
1    6   9       12     25
```

In this example:

- o The root node contains one key, **10**, and two child nodes.
- o The node with key **5** contains keys **1, 6, 9**, and the node with key **15** contains **12, 25**.
- o B-trees are designed so that each node has between **2** and **3 children** (depending on the order).

3. **Why B-Trees are Useful in Databases**:

167

- o **Efficient Indexing**: B-trees are used in databases for indexing purposes, where quick searching, insertion, and deletion are needed. The ability of B-trees to maintain balance ensures that these operations are performed efficiently, even with large datasets.

- o **Disk-Friendly**: Unlike binary search trees, B-trees are optimized for **disk storage**. Since each node can store multiple keys, fewer disk accesses are required to find the correct data, making B-trees particularly useful for systems where data is stored on disk (e.g., databases, file systems).

4. **Operations on B-Trees**:

- o **Insert**: To insert a new key, we start by finding the appropriate leaf node where the key should go. If the node has room for the new key, we insert it. If the node is full, we split it into two nodes and move the middle key up to the parent node.

- o **Search**: Searching in a B-tree is efficient because each node contains multiple keys, allowing us to skip over large portions of the tree with fewer comparisons.

- o **Delete**: Deletion in a B-tree is more complex. If the key to be deleted is in a leaf node, it is removed directly. If it is in an internal node, the

168

key is replaced with the largest key from the left subtree or the smallest key from the right subtree, and the tree is rebalanced if necessary.

Tries: Efficient Search and Retrieval of Strings

A **Trie** (pronounced as "try") is a tree-like data structure used to store a dynamic set of strings, often in the form of **prefix trees**. Each node in a trie represents a single character, and the edges represent possible character sequences. Tries are highly efficient for tasks like **autocomplete** and **dictionary lookups** because they allow for fast **prefix-based searches**.

1. **Trie Structure**:
   - A trie is a tree where each node represents a **character** in a string. The path from the root to any node represents a **prefix** of a string, and the leaf nodes represent complete strings.
   - The trie structure makes it easy to perform searches for strings that share common prefixes.

Example of a Trie:

```
css
Copy
    root
    /  \
   t    a
```

169

```
        /       \
      r           p
     / \         / \

i     e     p     p     /   \   /
enle
```

pgsql

Copy

In this example, the words **"tree"**, **"trap"**, and **"apple"** are stored in the trie. Notice how the nodes are shared for the common prefixes: "t" and "tr" are shared between "tree" and "trap".

2. **Real-World Applications**:

- **Dictionary Lookups**: Tries are used in many applications where fast lookups of words are required, such as spell checkers or dictionary-based search engines. Since tries store strings as paths, finding if a string exists in the dataset can be done in **O(m)** time, where `m` is the length of the string.

- **Autocomplete**: Tries are perfect for autocomplete systems where the user types a prefix, and the system needs to provide a list of words that match the given prefix.

3. **Operations on Tries**:

- **Insert**: To insert a string into a trie, we start at the root and insert each character of the string as we move down the tree. If a character node doesn't exist, we create a new node for it.
- **Search**: To search for a string, we follow the path that corresponds to the string's characters. If we reach the end of the string and a valid end node exists, the string is in the trie.
- **Delete**: Deletion in a trie is done by removing nodes that are no longer part of any string, ensuring that the trie remains compact.

Real-World Examples: Dictionary Lookups, Autocomplete Features

1. **Dictionary Lookups**:
- Tries are commonly used in applications that require **fast word lookups**, such as spell checkers and dictionary applications. Since a trie stores strings in a way that optimizes for **prefix-based searching**, finding whether a word exists in the dictionary can be done quickly.

Example: In a **text editor** or a **word processor**, a trie could be used to quickly check if a word exists in the dictionary,

171

enabling features like **auto-correction** and **spell-check**.

2. **Autocomplete Features**:
- Tries are used in **autocomplete systems**, where users type a few characters (a prefix), and the system returns a list of potential completions based on the prefix.
- When a user begins typing a word, the trie allows the system to efficiently find all words that start with that prefix, offering suggestions or completions.

Example: In **search engines** or **mobile keyboards**, the trie structure helps provide **real-time suggestions** based on the first few characters typed by the user.

Operations: Insert, Search, Delete

1. **Insert in Tries**:
- To insert a string into a trie, each character of the string is inserted as a node, starting from the root. If the character already exists in the trie, the algorithm simply moves to the next node. Otherwise, a new node is created for the character.

2. **Search in Tries**:

- To search for a string in a trie, we follow the path of nodes that corresponds to the string's characters. If we successfully traverse all characters of the string and reach the end node, the string exists in the trie.

3. **Delete in Tries**:
- To delete a string from a trie, we remove the nodes that are no longer part of any other string. If a node has no children and is not the end of any other word, it can be deleted. This ensures that the trie remains compact.

Summary of Key Points:

- **B-Trees** are a type of self-balancing search tree used for efficient indexing in databases and file systems. They are optimized for storage systems that read and write large blocks of data, and they ensure quick access to data by keeping the tree balanced and minimizing disk accesses.
- **Tries** are a specialized tree structure used for **efficient string storage and retrieval**, particularly for applications like **autocomplete** and **dictionary lookups**. They allow for fast prefix-based searches and are widely used in text-related applications.
- **B-tree operations** (insert, search, delete) are efficient, with time complexity **O(log n)**

for search operations, making them suitable for large-scale datasets.
- **Trie operations** (insert, search, delete) are efficient, with time complexity **O(m)**, where `m` is the length of the string being processed. This makes tries ideal for **real-time text-based applications** like autocomplete.

CHAPTER 18

ADVANCED GRAPH ALGORITHMS – FINDING THE .SHORTEST PATH

Dijkstra's Algorithm, Floyd-Warshall Algorithm, Bellman-Ford Algorithm

In the realm of graph theory, one of the most important problems is **finding the shortest path** between nodes in a graph. Whether it's for **navigation systems**, **network routing**, or **flight search engines**, algorithms that compute the shortest path have widespread applications in real-world systems. The three most widely used shortest path algorithms are **Dijkstra's Algorithm**, **Floyd-Warshall Algorithm**, and **Bellman-Ford Algorithm**. Let's dive into each of these algorithms and understand their workings, use cases, and time complexities.

1. Dijkstra's Algorithm

Dijkstra's Algorithm is one of the most efficient algorithms for finding the shortest path between a source node and all other nodes in a graph with non-negative edge weights. It is a **greedy algorithm**, meaning it iteratively selects the nearest node to the source and explores all its neighbors.

175

How it Works:

1. Initialize a **distance array** to store the shortest known distance from the source node to each node in the graph. Set the distance to the source node as 0 and all other nodes as infinity.

2. Mark all nodes as **unvisited**.

3. Set the current node to the source node.

4. For the current node, examine its unvisited neighbors and calculate their tentative distances. If the calculated distance is less than the current distance, update it.

5. Mark the current node as **visited**, meaning it will not be checked again.

6. Choose the unvisited node with the smallest tentative distance and set it as the new current node.

7. Repeat steps 4-6 until all nodes have been visited or the smallest tentative distance is infinity (meaning the remaining nodes are not connected to the source).

Real-World Example:

- **Navigation systems** like Google Maps use Dijkstra's algorithm to find the shortest driving route between two locations. Each location is a node, and roads between them are edges with associated weights (distances or travel times).

Time Complexity:

- Using an array for the priority queue: **O(V²)**, where V is the number of vertices.
- Using a binary heap: **O((V + E) log V)**, where E is the number of edges, and V is the number of vertices.
- **Space Complexity**: **O(V)**, as we need to store the distance of each vertex.

---

2. Floyd-Warshall Algorithm

The **Floyd-Warshall algorithm** is an all-pairs shortest path algorithm. Unlike Dijkstra's algorithm, which finds the shortest path from a source node to all other nodes, Floyd-Warshall computes the shortest paths between **every pair of nodes** in a graph. It can handle both **directed** and **undirected** graphs and works even when negative edge weights are present (provided there are no negative weight cycles).

How it Works:

1. Create a matrix `dist[][]` where `dist[i][j]` represents the shortest distance from node `i` to node `j`.

2. Initialize `dist[i][j]` to the weight of the edge between i and j, or infinity if no edge exists. Set `dist[i][i] = 0` for all nodes.

3. For each node `k` in the graph, update the matrix for all pairs of nodes (`i, j`) by checking if going from i to j through `k` is shorter than the current known distance (`dist[i][j]`):

$$dist[i][j]=\min(dist[i][j],dist[i][k]+dist[k][j])$$

4. Repeat this process for every node as an intermediate node.

5. After completing the algorithm, `dist[i][j]` will contain the shortest path from i to j.

Real-World Example:

- **Flight search engines** can use the Floyd-Warshall algorithm to find the shortest paths (minimum travel cost) between all airports in a network of flights. The algorithm computes the best possible routes from every airport to every other airport, which is crucial when users search for flights between multiple destinations.

Time Complexity:

- **Time Complexity**: **O(V³)**, where V is the number of vertices (nodes). This is because we iterate through all pairs of nodes for every possible intermediate node.
- **Space Complexity**: **O(V²)**, as we need to store the distance matrix.

---

3. Bellman-Ford Algorithm

The **Bellman-Ford algorithm** is another shortest path algorithm that is useful when the graph contains **negative edge weights**. Unlike Dijkstra's algorithm, Bellman-Ford can handle graphs with negative weights, but it does not work with graphs containing negative weight cycles (where the total sum of the cycle is negative, leading to infinitely decreasing path lengths).

How it Works:

1. Initialize the distance to the source node as 0 and the distance to all other nodes as infinity.
2. For each edge in the graph, check if the path through that edge offers a shorter path to the destination node. If it does, update the distance.
3. Repeat this process **V-1** times, where V is the number of vertices. This ensures that the shortest path is found, as

179

the maximum number of edges in any shortest path is $V-1$.

4. After $V-1$ iterations, check for negative weight cycles by running through the edges again. If any distance can still be relaxed, then a negative weight cycle exists.

Real-World Example:

- **Negative weight cycles** can occur in **financial applications** or **currency exchange systems**, where currency exchanges might involve conversion rates that lead to cycles of exchange with decreasing value. Bellman-Ford is used to detect such cycles and handle negative weights in these applications.

Time Complexity:

- **Time Complexity: O(V * E)**, where V is the number of vertices and E is the number of edges. This is because we relax all edges **V-1 times**.
- **Space Complexity: O(V)**, as we need to store the distances of all vertices.

Real-World Applications: Navigation Systems, Route Planning

1. **Navigation Systems**:

   o **Dijkstra's algorithm** is commonly used in **GPS systems** and **navigation software** to find the shortest driving, walking, or cycling routes between two points on a map. The graph nodes represent locations, and the edges represent roads with weights corresponding to distances or travel times.

2. **Route Planning**:

   o **Floyd-Warshall** can be useful in **multi-destination route planning** (e.g., when finding optimal routes between several locations). This algorithm is especially helpful when the system needs to compute all pairwise shortest paths in a city or transportation network.

3. **Networking**:

   o **Shortest path algorithms** are heavily used in **networking** for routing packets between nodes (routers) on the internet. **Bellman-Ford** is often used in **distance vector routing** protocols, where each router calculates the shortest path to every other router in the network.

4. **Flight Search Engines**:

   o Algorithms like **Floyd-Warshall** help in **flight search engines** to determine the best routes between multiple airports, accounting for all possible connections between cities and optimizing the search for the lowest-cost flight.

Time Complexity Analysis

Here's a summary of the time complexities for the discussed algorithms:

Algorithm	Time Complexity	Space Complexity
Dijkstra's	$O((V + E) \log V)$	$O(V)$
Floyd-Warshall	$O(V^3)$	$O(V^2)$
Bellman-Ford	$O(V * E)$	$O(V)$

- **Dijkstra's Algorithm** is the most efficient for graphs with non-negative weights when using a **priority queue**.
- **Floyd-Warshall** has a cubic time complexity and is better for **all-pairs shortest path problems**.
- **Bellman-Ford** is slower but essential for handling **graphs with negative weights**.

Summary of Key Points:

- **Dijkstra's algorithm** is efficient for finding the shortest path from a source to all other nodes in a graph with non-negative edge weights. It's widely used in applications like **navigation systems**.

- **Floyd-Warshall algorithm** is used for **all-pairs shortest path problems** and is useful for applications like **flight search engines**, where the shortest paths between multiple destinations are needed.

- **Bellman-Ford algorithm** is crucial for graphs with **negative edge weights** and can also be used to **detect negative weight cycles**, making it ideal for applications like **currency exchange** and **networking**.

- **Time complexity analysis** varies by algorithm, with Dijkstra's being the most efficient for graphs with positive weights and Floyd-Warshall being ideal for small graphs where all pairs of shortest paths are required.

CHAPTER 19

NETWORK FLOW ALGORITHMS – MANAGING DATA FLOW

Max-Flow Min-Cut Theorem and Ford-Fulkerson Algorithm

Network Flow Algorithms are essential for solving problems where resources are being transferred through a network, such as **data transmission**, **resource allocation**, and **transportation planning**. One of the most important concepts in this area is the **Max-Flow Min-Cut Theorem**, which underpins several key algorithms, including the **Ford-Fulkerson algorithm**. These algorithms are widely used in **computer networks**, **supply chain management**, and **transportation logistics**.

Max-Flow Min-Cut Theorem

The **Max-Flow Min-Cut Theorem** is a fundamental result in network flow theory. It relates two important concepts in the flow network: **maximum flow** and **minimum cut**.

- **Max-flow**: The maximum amount of flow that can be pushed from the **source node** to the **sink node** in a network, given the capacities of the edges.

- **Min-cut**: The smallest total capacity of the edges that, if removed, would disconnect the source from the sink. This cut essentially "cuts off" the flow.

The **Max-Flow Min-Cut Theorem** states that:

The **maximum flow** in a network is equal to the **minimum cut** of the network.

This theorem provides a way to measure the maximum flow in a network and helps in identifying bottlenecks where the flow is limited.

Key Insights:

1. If you have a network of pipes with limited capacity, the **maximum flow** corresponds to the greatest amount of liquid that can flow from the start to the end of the system.
2. The **minimum cut** represents the smallest collection of pipes whose removal would stop the flow entirely.

Ford-Fulkerson Algorithm

The **Ford-Fulkerson algorithm** is a method used to find the **maximum flow** in a flow network. It uses **augmenting paths** to

185

push flow through the network, improving the flow until no more augmenting paths can be found.

How Ford-Fulkerson Algorithm Works:

1. **Initialization**: Start with zero flow on all edges of the network.

2. **Find Augmenting Path**: Search for a path from the source to the sink that can carry more flow (an augmenting path). This path must have available capacity on each edge along the way.

3. **Increase Flow**: Once an augmenting path is found, push as much flow as possible along this path. This is done by increasing the flow along the edges in the path and decreasing the flow capacity of these edges.

4. **Repeat**: Repeat the process of finding augmenting paths and increasing the flow until no more augmenting paths can be found.

5. **Termination**: When no more augmenting paths are available, the flow is at its maximum.

Important Note: The Ford-Fulkerson algorithm can run into problems with **infinite loops** in the case of **fractional capacities** (real-number capacities). To avoid this, we typically use **Edmonds-Karp** (a specific implementation of Ford-Fulkerson using BFS) or **capacity scaling** for efficiency.

Example of Ford-Fulkerson:

Suppose we have a simple network with nodes S (source), A, B, and T (sink), with the following capacities:

```rust
Copy
    S --(10)-> A --(5)-> T
    |          |         ^
    v          v         |
    B --(10)-> T --(10)-> |
```

Step-by-step:

1. Initially, the flow is zero.
2. Find an augmenting path: S -> A -> T with capacity 5 (minimum capacity along the path).
3. Push 5 units of flow along S -> A -> T.
4. Update capacities:
   o   S -> A becomes 5.
   o   A -> T becomes 0.
   o   B -> T becomes 5 (due to available capacity).
5. Repeat the process until no more augmenting paths are found.

Time Complexity:

187

- The time complexity depends on how we find augmenting paths. In the worst case, the time complexity is **O(max_flow * E)**, where E is the number of edges and `max_flow` is the maximum flow in the network.

Real-World Examples: Data Transmission and Resource Allocation

1. **Data Transmission**:
   - o In **computer networks**, the Max-Flow Min-Cut theorem is often used to model and optimize data transmission. For example, the network could represent routers and links between them, with the edges having certain capacities (maximum bandwidth). The Ford-Fulkerson algorithm or similar algorithms are used to determine the maximum possible data transfer rate between two nodes (such as from a server to a client).

   Example: In a **data center** or **cloud computing network**, data is transmitted through a series of routers, and algorithms like Ford-Fulkerson are used to calculate the maximum possible bandwidth available between any two nodes in the network, ensuring efficient use of resources.

2. **Resource Allocation**:

   o In **resource allocation** problems, the Max-Flow Min-Cut theorem can be applied to ensure the most efficient use of limited resources. For example, consider the allocation of **water flow** through a network of pipes, or **traffic routing** in cities.

   Example: A **manufacturing facility** may use Max-Flow algorithms to allocate resources (like raw materials or machinery time) efficiently across different production lines to maximize output. The **minimum cut** in the network might represent the capacity limit that constrains overall production.

Use Cases in Computer Networks and Transportation

1. **Computer Networks**:

   o **Bandwidth Allocation**: In computer networks, Max-Flow algorithms are used to allocate bandwidth between different nodes (servers, routers) while ensuring optimal performance. For instance, in a **data center**, algorithms can help balance the load across servers by adjusting the data flow to prevent congestion and maximize throughput.

o **Routing and Traffic Management**: In communication networks, **network flow algorithms** help in designing routing protocols to ensure that the traffic between various nodes is optimized. This could involve finding paths that minimize delays or maximize bandwidth usage.

2. **Transportation Networks**:

o **Traffic Flow Management**: In transportation networks, such as **road systems** or **airline routes**, the Max-Flow algorithm can model traffic flow and help optimize the allocation of resources like road lanes, flight routes, or cargo space in a way that minimizes delays and maximizes throughput.

o **Airline Scheduling**: In the airline industry, algorithms like Ford-Fulkerson can help in managing flight schedules, optimizing routes, and determining the maximum number of passengers that can be accommodated from one city to another, taking into account constraints such as available aircraft capacity.

Implementing Algorithms in Practice

1. **Data Structures**:
   - To implement network flow algorithms, efficient data structures are required:
     - **Adjacency Matrix** or **Adjacency List**: Used to represent the graph, where nodes represent entities (routers, cities, etc.), and edges represent the capacity between them.
     - **Residual Graph**: A graph that holds the residual capacities (remaining flow) after each augmentation.

2. **Practical Considerations**:
   - In practice, Ford-Fulkerson is implemented with an **augmenting path search** (usually using **Breadth-First Search (BFS)** in **Edmonds-Karp** or **Depth-First Search (DFS)** for other variations).
   - **Cycle Detection**: It's essential to ensure that the graph does not have any negative weight cycles (as in the Bellman-Ford algorithm), which would lead to infinite flows.

Time Complexity Analysis

The time complexity of these algorithms can vary significantly depending on the specific implementation:

Algorithm	Time Complexity	Space Complexity
Ford-Fulkerson	$O(max\_flow * E)$ (worst case)	$O(V + E)$
Edmonds-Karp (BFS)	$O(V * E^2)$	$O(V + E)$
Floyd-Warshall	$O(V^3)$	$O(V^2)$

- **Ford-Fulkerson**'s time complexity depends on the maximum flow in the graph. The **Edmonds-Karp implementation** (which uses BFS) improves this by using a **polynomial time complexity**.
- **Floyd-Warshall** has $O(V^3)$ complexity and is more suited for **all-pairs shortest path** problems rather than flow optimization.

Summary of Key Points:

- **Network flow algorithms**, including the **Ford-Fulkerson algorithm, Max-Flow Min-Cut Theorem**, and **Edmonds-Karp**, are essential for solving real-world problems involving the allocation of resources, data transmission, and optimization of network flow.

- **Ford-Fulkerson** is effective for finding the **maximum flow** in networks with non-negative capacities, while **Floyd-Warshall** is better suited for finding **all-pairs shortest paths**.

- **Real-world applications** include **data transmission in computer networks**, **resource allocation in manufacturing**, and **traffic flow management in transportation**.

- Efficient implementation of these algorithms requires the use of **adjacency matrices or lists** and the maintenance of a **residual graph** for flow adjustments.

CHAPTER 20

STRING ALGORITHMS –
MASTERING TEXT PROCESSING

String Matching Algorithms: Knuth-Morris-Pratt, Rabin-Karp

String matching algorithms are crucial for efficiently finding substrings or patterns within a larger string. They are foundational to many applications like **search engines**, **text editors**, **plagiarism detection**, and **data mining**. Two of the most important string matching algorithms are the **Knuth-Morris-Pratt (KMP)** algorithm and the **Rabin-Karp** algorithm. Each algorithm has its own approach and use cases, depending on the problem at hand.

---

1. Knuth-Morris-Pratt (KMP) Algorithm

The **Knuth-Morris-Pratt** (KMP) algorithm is an efficient string-matching algorithm that improves upon the naive brute-force approach. The main idea of KMP is to avoid unnecessary re-examination of characters that have already been matched.

How KMP Works:

1. **Preprocessing**:
   - KMP first preprocesses the **pattern** (the string we are trying to match) to create a **partial match table** (also known as the **failure function**). This table helps in determining the next position to compare when a mismatch occurs, without revisiting already checked characters.

2. **Pattern Matching**:
   - During the matching phase, the algorithm checks characters one by one. If there's a mismatch, instead of starting from the beginning of the pattern, KMP uses the failure function to shift the pattern to the right efficiently, skipping over parts of the string that have already been checked.

3. **Failure Function**:
   - The failure function tells us, for each position in the pattern, the length of the longest proper prefix of the pattern that is also a suffix. This helps the algorithm to skip redundant comparisons.

Time Complexity:

- **Preprocessing time**: $O(m)$, where m is the length of the pattern.
- **Matching time**: $O(n)$, where n is the length of the text.

- **Overall Time Complexity**: **O(n + m)**, making KMP one of the most efficient string matching algorithms for large inputs.

Real-World Example:

- **Search Engines**: When performing a search, KMP can efficiently search for the query term (pattern) within a large collection of indexed web pages (text), ensuring that the search results are returned quickly.

2. Rabin-Karp Algorithm

The **Rabin-Karp** algorithm is another popular string matching algorithm that uses **hashing** to quickly identify potential matches between the pattern and substrings of the text. It is particularly effective when you are looking for multiple patterns in a text.

How Rabin-Karp Works:

1. **Hash Function**:
   - The algorithm computes a hash value for the pattern and for all **substrings of the text** that are of the same length as the pattern. The **hash function** calculates a unique value for each substring based on its characters.

196

2. **Matching**:

   o   After calculating the hash values, Rabin-Karp compares the hash value of the pattern to the hash value of substrings in the text. If the hash values match, it then checks the actual substring to confirm the match.

3. **Rolling Hash**:

   o   Rabin-Karp uses a **rolling hash** function to efficiently compute the hash values of the substrings. The rolling hash allows the hash value of the substring to be updated incrementally as the window slides over the text, without needing to recalculate the hash from scratch for each new substring.

Time Complexity:

- **Worst-case time complexity**: **O(n * m)**, where n is the length of the text and m is the length of the pattern. This occurs when there are many hash collisions.
- **Average-case time complexity**: **O(n + m)**, assuming that the hash function distributes values uniformly and there are few collisions.

Real-World Example:

- **Plagiarism Detection**: Rabin-Karp can be used to detect plagiarism by searching for multiple substrings (e.g., phrases or sentences) in a large body of text. If multiple substrings in the text have the same hash value, it suggests that the same phrases appear in both texts.

Applications: Pattern Matching, Text Searching

String matching algorithms like KMP and Rabin-Karp have a wide range of applications in both text processing and other domains involving string data. Some of the most common applications include:

1. **Pattern Matching**:
   - In **data mining** and **information retrieval**, string matching algorithms are used to find specific patterns or sequences within larger datasets. This can be useful for identifying keywords or phrases within large bodies of text, logs, or datasets.
2. **Text Searching**:
   - **Text editors** and **search engines** rely on string matching algorithms to allow users to search for specific words or phrases within documents, web

pages, or large datasets. KMP and Rabin-Karp are often used in this context to provide fast search results.

3. **Plagiarism Detection**:
   o **Plagiarism detection software** uses string matching algorithms to identify similarities between documents. By looking for substrings that match between documents, the software can flag possible instances of copied content.

4. **Bioinformatics**:
   o In **bioinformatics**, string matching algorithms are used to compare DNA sequences, identify genetic markers, and search for patterns in large genomic data sets. These algorithms help find matches between DNA sequences and can identify mutations, genes, and other genetic information.

5. **Spam Filtering**:
   o String matching algorithms are also used in **spam filtering** to identify potentially malicious or unwanted content by searching for specific patterns or phrases commonly found in spam emails.

Time Complexity and Optimizations

Knuth-Morris-Pratt (KMP) Time Complexity:

- **Preprocessing**: **O(m)**, where m is the length of the pattern.
- **Matching**: **O(n)**, where n is the length of the text.
- **Overall Complexity**: **O(n + m)**.

Rabin-Karp Time Complexity:

- **Worst-case**: **O(n * m)** due to hash collisions.
- **Average-case**: **O(n + m)** with a good hash function that minimizes collisions.

Optimizations:

1. **KMP**: The failure function can be precomputed in **O(m)** time, and once this is done, the matching phase proceeds in **O(n)** time, making KMP one of the fastest algorithms for single-pattern matching.
2. **Rabin-Karp**: The **rolling hash** function allows Rabin-Karp to efficiently calculate the hash for all substrings, making it more suitable for cases where we need to search for multiple patterns at once. The worst-case time complexity can be improved using better hash functions to reduce collisions.

Summary of Key Points:

- **String matching algorithms** like **Knuth-Morris-Pratt (KMP)** and **Rabin-Karp** provide efficient methods for finding substrings or patterns within a larger text.

- **KMP** avoids redundant comparisons by preprocessing the pattern to create a failure function, making it efficient for single-pattern matching with a time complexity of $O(n + m)$.

- **Rabin-Karp** uses **hashing** to quickly identify potential matches and is effective when searching for **multiple patterns**. Its worst-case time complexity is $O(n * m)$, but the average-case is much better with a good hash function.

- **Real-world examples** include **search engines**, **plagiarism detection**, **bioinformatics**, and **text searching** in text editors.

- Optimizations such as the **rolling hash** in Rabin-Karp and the **failure function** in KMP help reduce time complexity and improve performance.

CHAPTER 21

COMPUTATIONAL GEOMETRY – PROBLEM SOLVING IN GEOMETRY

Understanding Geometric Algorithms

Computational Geometry is the study of algorithms that deal with **geometrical objects** and solve problems related to **geometry**. This field is crucial for areas such as **computer graphics**, **robotics**, **computer-aided design (CAD)**, and **geographical information systems (GIS)**. The primary goal of computational geometry is to design algorithms that are both **efficient** and **accurate** when handling geometric data, such as points, lines, polygons, and other shapes.

Some common **geometrical objects** in computational geometry include:

- **Points**: Defined by coordinates in a 2D or 3D space.
- **Lines and Line Segments**: Straight lines, either infinite or bounded by two endpoints.
- **Polygons**: Closed shapes made by connecting a series of line segments.
- **Circles**: Defined by a center and radius.

Geometric algorithms are designed to **process these objects** and solve problems such as finding the **intersection** of two lines, calculating the **area of a polygon**, or determining the **closest points** in a set of points.

Real-World Examples: Collision Detection, GPS Routing

1. **Collision Detection**:
   - In **games** and **simulations, collision detection** algorithms are used to determine when two objects (e.g., a player and an obstacle in a game, or two vehicles in a simulation) collide. These algorithms help in preventing objects from passing through each other and ensure realistic interaction in virtual environments.
   - **Example**: In **3D games**, detecting when a character's bounding box intersects with the environment, or when two moving objects cross each other's paths, can be solved using computational geometry algorithms.

   Algorithms:

- o **Bounding Box**: A simple method where we enclose objects within a rectangular box and check for overlaps between these boxes.
- o **Separating Axis Theorem (SAT)**: A more sophisticated method for polygon and 3D model collision detection that ensures objects are separated along various axes.

2. **GPS Routing**:

- o **GPS systems** rely heavily on geometric algorithms to determine the **shortest path** between two points on the Earth's surface. These algorithms must handle **geodesic distances** and obstacles (e.g., roads, rivers) and optimize for **fastest** or **shortest** travel routes.
- o **Example**: In **GPS navigation**, **Dijkstra's algorithm** or *A search** is used to calculate the most efficient route from a starting point to a destination, considering road networks as a graph and intersections as nodes.

Geometric algorithms are used in preprocessing the map and in dynamically adjusting the route as new data becomes available (e.g., traffic conditions, road closures).

Basic Problems: Convex Hull, Closest Pair of Points

1. **Convex Hull**:
   - **Problem**: Given a set of points in the plane, the **convex hull** is the smallest convex polygon that encloses all the points.
   - **Convex Hull Algorithms**:
     - **Graham's Scan**: Sorts the points by angle and constructs the convex hull in **O(n log n)** time.
     - **Jarvis's March (Gift Wrapping)**: Starts with the leftmost point and repeatedly selects the next point that forms the smallest angle with the current point. This algorithm runs in **O(nh)** time, where h is the number of points in the convex hull.
   - **Real-World Example**: The convex hull is used in **robotics** for path planning, where a robot needs to navigate around obstacles. The convex hull can represent the boundary of free space, and the robot can plan its path around this boundary.

   Applications:

o **Computational Geometry**: In geometric shape recognition, the convex hull helps in identifying the boundary of a shape.

o **Geographic Mapping**: Convex hull algorithms are used in mapping systems to identify areas of interest (e.g., the area within a region).

2. **Closest Pair of Points**:

o **Problem**: Given a set of points in a 2D plane, find the pair of points that are closest to each other.

o **Naive Approach**: A simple approach would be to check the distance between every possible pair of points, which has a time complexity of $O(n^2)$.

o **Efficient Approach**: The **divide and conquer** algorithm can solve this problem in $O(n \log n)$ time by recursively dividing the points into halves and merging them while checking for closer points across the dividing line.

Applications:

o **Geospatial Systems**: In geographic systems, finding the closest pair of points is useful for determining the nearest facilities (e.g., hospitals, gas stations) to a given location.

o **Image Processing**: The closest pair of points algorithm can be used in image matching and feature recognition.

Applications in Games and Simulations

Computational geometry plays a crucial role in the development of **games** and **simulations**, as these systems often rely on complex geometric calculations to simulate real-world behavior and interactions. Some of the most important applications of computational geometry in games and simulations include:

1. **Pathfinding**:
   - Algorithms like *A search** use geometric algorithms to find the shortest or fastest path between points on a map, factoring in obstacles and terrain types. For example, in a **real-time strategy (RTS) game**, units might need to navigate around mountains, forests, or buildings, and geometric algorithms help calculate the optimal path.

2. **Collision Detection**:
   - In **3D games** or **physics simulations**, geometric algorithms are used to detect when two objects collide. These algorithms determine if the bounding boxes, spheres, or polygons of objects intersect and compute the point and angle of collision.

3. **Mesh Generation and Processing**:

- o **3D rendering** in games and simulations often involves **mesh generation**, where the environment and objects are represented as meshes (a collection of vertices, edges, and faces). Computational geometry algorithms are used to process and refine these meshes for rendering and physical simulations.

4. **Simulation of Real-World Phenomena**:
   - o Computational geometry is used to simulate **natural phenomena** like the flow of water, erosion, or the movement of particles in space. Geometric algorithms help model the interaction of particles, terrains, or fluids in virtual environments.

5. **Geographical Mapping and Terrain Modeling**:
   - o In **geographic information systems (GIS)** or **simulation of outdoor environments**, computational geometry is used to model the terrain and landscape. Algorithms like the **convex hull** and **Voronoi diagrams** can be used to model terrain boundaries and regions of influence for various features (e.g., cities, rivers).

Time Complexity and Optimizations

1. **Convex Hull Algorithms**:
   - **Graham's Scan**: **O(n log n)**, where n is the number of points.
   - **Jarvis's March (Gift Wrapping)**: **O(nh)**, where n is the number of points and h is the number of points in the convex hull.

2. **Closest Pair of Points**:
   - **Naive Approach**: **O(n²)**, where n is the number of points.
   - **Divide and Conquer Approach**: **O(n log n)**, which is much more efficient than the naive approach.

3. **General Time Complexity Considerations**:
   - Computational geometry problems often involve **divide and conquer** strategies, which lead to **O(n log n)** time complexity in many cases. However, some problems may require more specialized optimizations, such as **sweeping line algorithms**, **dynamic programming**, or **advanced data structures** like **segment trees** and **quadtrees** to improve performance.

Summary of Key Points:

- **Computational geometry** is the field of algorithms that deal with geometric objects and solve geometry-related problems efficiently. It is widely used in areas like **robotics, computer graphics, geographic information systems (GIS)**, and **game development**.

- **Basic problems** like the **convex hull** and the **closest pair of points** are fundamental to computational geometry and have numerous real-world applications, such as **collision detection, GPS routing**, and **plagiarism detection**.

- **Applications** in **games and simulations** involve **pathfinding, collision detection**, and **mesh generation**, all of which depend on efficient geometric algorithms.

- **Time complexity** for basic geometric algorithms is typically **O(n log n)**, but optimization techniques like **divide and conquer** or advanced data structures can improve efficiency.

Computational geometry is an essential part of computer science that has a direct impact on many fields, making problems related to geometry more tractable and solvable in real-time applications.

CHAPTER 22

DISJOINT SET UNION (UNION-FIND) – GROUPING DATA EFFICIENTLY

Introduction to Union-Find Data Structure

The **Union-Find** data structure, also known as **Disjoint Set Union (DSU)**, is a powerful data structure used to efficiently manage and track a collection of disjoint sets. It supports two primary operations:

1. **Union**: This operation merges two sets into a single set.
2. **Find**: This operation determines which set a particular element belongs to.

The Union-Find structure is widely used in solving problems related to **network connectivity, graph algorithms**, and **equivalence relations**. It allows these operations to be performed very efficiently, even with large datasets, making it an essential tool for various computational problems.

The structure keeps track of the **sets of elements** and supports efficient **union** and **find** operations. Over time, optimizations like **path compression** and **union by rank** (or size) have made the

211

Union-Find data structure one of the most efficient ways to solve problems involving disjoint sets.

Real-World Example: Social Networks, Connectivity Problems

The **Union-Find** data structure is particularly useful in **social networks**, **network connectivity**, and scenarios where we need to determine if two elements are in the same set or group. Here are a few real-world examples:

1. **Social Networks**:
   - In social networks like **Facebook**, **Twitter**, or **LinkedIn**, the Union-Find data structure can be used to find if two users are in the same group or connected. For example, if two users are friends, the system would group them together. If a new friendship is formed, we perform a **union** operation to connect the two sets.

   Example: If we want to determine if two users are connected (directly or indirectly), we can perform a **find** operation on both users to check if they belong to the same group. If they do, they are connected; if not, we **union** their groups.

212

2. **Connectivity Problems**:

   o In **network design** or **communication networks**, Union-Find is used to check whether two nodes (routers, computers, etc.) are connected or to merge two networks into a larger one. For example, checking if two websites are in the same **connected component** or determining if all nodes are connected in a **spanning tree**.

   Example: In **network connectivity**, if a new link between two routers is added, the Union-Find structure can help in efficiently determining whether adding this link connects two previously disjoint network components. If they are already connected, no action is needed; otherwise, the two components are merged using the **union** operation.

Operations: Find, Union, Path Compression

The **Union-Find** data structure revolves around two main operations:

213

1. Find Operation

The **Find** operation determines which set an element belongs to. This is often referred to as determining the **representative** or **leader** of the set containing the element.

Optimizations:

- **Path Compression**: In a naïve Union-Find structure, the `Find` operation could involve traversing up a tree (or chain of linked sets) to find the root, which could be slow. **Path compression** optimizes this by flattening the structure during the find operation, ensuring that future `Find` operations are faster.

How it Works:

1. Start at the node and follow the parent pointers until you reach the **root** (representative).
2. Optionally apply **path compression** to make all nodes along the path point directly to the root.

```python
Copy
def find(parent, x):
    if parent[x] != x:
        parent[x] = find(parent, parent[x])   #
Path compression
    return parent[x]
```

2. Union Operation

The **Union** operation merges two sets into one. It is often used after a `Find` operation determines that two elements belong to different sets. The goal is to **combine** these two sets into one set.

Optimizations:

- **Union by Rank (or Size)**: Instead of simply linking one tree to another, we always attach the smaller tree (or the tree with lower rank/size) to the root of the larger tree. This keeps the tree shallow and ensures that the **Find** operation remains efficient.

How it Works:

1. Find the roots of both sets.
2. If the roots are different, merge the two sets by linking one root to the other.
3. If the **union by rank** is applied, attach the root with smaller rank (or size) to the root with the larger rank.

```python
Copy
def union(parent, rank, x, y):
    rootX = find(parent, x)
    rootY = find(parent, y)

    if rootX != rootY:
```

```
# Union by rank
if rank[rootX] > rank[rootY]:
    parent[rootY] = rootX
elif rank[rootX] < rank[rootY]:
    parent[rootX] = rootY
else:
    parent[rootY] = rootX
    rank[rootX] += 1
```

3. Path Compression and Union by Rank

- **Path Compression**: Path compression ensures that each Find operation takes **O(log n)** or better by flattening the tree structure. This speeds up future operations by ensuring that the trees remain shallow.

- **Union by Rank**: Union by rank ensures that the trees are balanced, preventing them from becoming too deep and thus maintaining efficient operations.

Applications in Network Connectivity and Kruskal's Algorithm

1. **Network Connectivity**:
   o The Union-Find data structure is used extensively in **network connectivity** problems, where we need to efficiently determine if two nodes are

216

connected or if adding a new edge will connect previously disconnected components.

- o **Example**: In a **dynamic network**, if a new connection (edge) between two routers is added, we can check if the routers are already connected by calling the `Find` operation. If they are not connected, we use the `Union` operation to merge their respective sets.

2. **Kruskal's Algorithm**:

- o **Kruskal's algorithm** is a well-known **minimum spanning tree (MST)** algorithm that uses Union-Find to efficiently handle the merging of different components of the graph. In Kruskal's algorithm, edges are processed in increasing order of weight, and the Union-Find structure is used to check if adding an edge would create a cycle. If it does, the edge is skipped; otherwise, the edge is added to the MST by performing the `Union` operation.

Steps in Kruskal's Algorithm:

2. Sort all edges by weight.

3. Initialize a Union-Find structure to keep track of connected components.

4. For each edge, check if it connects two different components using the `Find` operation.

217

5. If they are not connected, add the edge to the MST and perform the `Union` operation.

6. Repeat until all edges are processed or the MST is complete.

Time Complexity:

○ Sorting the edges takes **O(E log E)**, and each union/find operation takes **O(α(n))**, where α(n) is the inverse Ackermann function (which grows extremely slowly and is nearly constant for all practical values of n).

○ The overall time complexity of Kruskal's algorithm is **O(E log E)**, where E is the number of edges.

Real-World Use Cases

1. **Social Networks**:
   ○ Union-Find is used to group users into **connected components**, where each component represents a group of users who are directly or indirectly connected.
   ○ **Example**: If two users **A** and **B** are friends (directly or indirectly), they are part of the same

connected component. When a new connection is made, the Union-Find data structure helps efficiently merge the two sets.

2. **Network Connectivity**:
   o Union-Find is often used in **network design** to maintain the connectivity of different nodes in the network, ensuring efficient management of resources and preventing network failures.
   o **Example**: In computer networks, routers and nodes are connected by edges (communication channels). The Union-Find structure helps determine whether adding a new connection will cause any cycles (redundant paths).

3. **MST (Minimum Spanning Tree) in Kruskal's Algorithm**:
   o Union-Find is widely used in **graph theory**, specifically in **minimum spanning tree** problems. **Kruskal's algorithm** utilizes Union-Find to efficiently determine if two nodes are part of the same tree before adding an edge to the spanning tree.

Example: In **network design**, you might use Kruskal's algorithm with Union-Find to connect cities with the minimum cost of laying down communication lines.

Time Complexity and Optimizations

- **Find** and **Union** operations are optimized with **path compression** and **union by rank**, leading to nearly constant time complexity:
    - **Time Complexity**: Each operation (Find and Union) has $O(\alpha(n))$ time complexity, where $\alpha(n)$ is the inverse Ackermann function.
    - **Space Complexity**: $O(n)$, as we need to store the parent and rank arrays for all elements.

Summary of Key Points:

- The **Union-Find** data structure is a powerful tool for efficiently managing disjoint sets and solving problems related to connectivity, grouping, and equivalence relations.
- **Key operations** include Find (determining the representative of a set) and Union (merging two sets), optimized by **path compression** and **union by rank** to ensure near-constant time operations.
- **Real-world applications** include **social networks**, **network connectivity**, and **Kruskal's algorithm** for finding **minimum spanning trees**.

220

- The Union-Find data structure plays a vital role in efficiently solving graph-related problems, including **minimum spanning tree problems, dynamic connectivity problems**, and **grouping and clustering** tasks.

CHAPTER 23

AMORTIZED ANALYSIS – ANALYZING AVERAGE CASE PERFORMANCE

Introduction to Amortized Analysis and When to Use It

Amortized analysis is a technique used to analyze the **average performance** of an algorithm over a **sequence of operations**, rather than considering the time complexity of a single operation in isolation. This is particularly useful when an algorithm has operations that vary in time complexity—some operations are very fast, while others may take much longer. In such cases, amortized analysis helps to understand the **average time complexity** per operation when multiple operations are considered together.

Why Use Amortized Analysis?

- **Variable Time Costs**: Some algorithms or data structures have operations that involve both **cheap** and **expensive** steps. Amortized analysis helps in determining the **average time complexity** per operation over the long run.
- **Real-World Performance**: It provides a more accurate estimate of an algorithm's overall performance,

particularly when it's important to analyze the total time over many operations.

- **Avoids Worst-Case Focus**: Unlike worst-case analysis, which assumes the **worst** scenario for every operation, amortized analysis looks at the **average case** over multiple operations, giving a more representative measure of real-world performance.

Amortized analysis is often used in scenarios where operations may seem inefficient in isolation but become efficient when averaged over many operations.

Real-World Examples: Stack Resizing, Dynamic Arrays

1. **Stack Resizing**:
   - **Stack** operations typically involve pushing and popping elements. In most cases, the **push** operation takes constant time **O(1)**, but occasionally, the stack must be **resized** when it reaches its capacity. Resizing requires **O(n)** time, where n is the number of elements currently in the stack.

   Amortized Analysis of Stack Resizing:
   - Suppose the stack doubles in size whenever it becomes full. While resizing is an expensive

operation, it only occurs when the stack reaches its capacity, which is less frequent as the stack grows. If you consider the **total cost of resizing** across many operations, the average cost per operation (amortized cost) becomes much lower.

Example:

- o Let's say you have a stack of size 1, and every time it fills up, it doubles its size. Over a sequence of operations, resizing happens less and less frequently. By amortizing the costs, the **amortized time complexity** of the push operation is **O(1)**, even though resizing takes **O(n)** time when it occurs.

- o If you perform k operations, the total cost will involve several costly resizing steps, but over the entire sequence of k operations, the average cost per operation is much lower.

- o **Amortized Time Complexity**: **O(1)** for each push, even though resizing takes **O(n)** in the worst case.

2. **Dynamic Arrays**:
   - o **Dynamic arrays** (like Python's **list** or **Java's ArrayList**) automatically resize when they run out of space. When the array reaches its capacity, a new larger array is allocated, and all elements

are copied to the new array. This resize operation takes **O(n)** time. However, most insertions happen in **O(1)** time, since no resizing is required.

Amortized Analysis of Dynamic Array Resizing:

o   Just like stack resizing, the **resizing cost** in a dynamic array is paid only occasionally, so the **average cost** per insertion is **O(1)**, even though resizing itself is **O(n)** in the worst case.

Example:

o   Suppose you have an array of size 1, and each time it becomes full, its size is doubled. Over a sequence of insertions, the resizing happens less frequently, and the amortized time complexity of insertion is **O(1)**.

o   **Amortized Time Complexity**: **O(1)** per insertion on average, despite occasional **O(n)** resizing.

Amortized Time Complexity: Examples with Real Data

To better understand **amortized time complexity**, let's look at an example using **dynamic arrays** and **stack resizing**:

1. **Dynamic Array Resizing Example**:
   - Let's say we start with an array of size 1, and it doubles its size whenever it fills up. The number of operations until the array is resized depends on the current size of the array.
   - Suppose we perform k insertions:
       1. **Insertion 1**: Takes **O(1)**.
       2. **Insertion 2**: Takes **O(1)**.
       3. **Insertion 3**: Resizes the array and takes **O(2)**.
       4. **Insertion 4**: Takes **O(1)** after resizing.
       5. **Insertion 5**: Takes **O(1)**.
       6. **Insertion 6**: Resizes the array and takes **O(4)**.
   - Total cost for k = 8 insertions would be:

   $$O(1)+O(1)+O(2)+O(1)+O(1)+O(4)+O(1)+O(1)=$$
   $$O(11)O(1) + O(1) + O(2) + O(1) + O(1) + O(4) + O(1) + O(1) =$$
   $$O(11)O(1)+O(1)+O(2)+O(1)+O(1)+O(4)+O(1)+O(1)=O(11)$$

       - The **total cost** is **O(11)** for k = 8 insertions.
   - The **amortized time per operation** is:

O(11)/8=O(1.375)O(11)   /   8   =
O(1.375)O(11)/8=O(1.375)

- **Amortized Cost**: As we perform more insertions, the **average cost** per insertion approaches **O(1)**.

2. **Stack Resizing Example**:
    o If a stack doubles in size every time it reaches capacity, the sequence of operations might look like this:
        0. **Push 1**: Takes **O(1)**.
        1. **Push 2**: Takes **O(1)**.
        2. **Push 3**: Resizes and takes **O(2)**.
        3. **Push 4**: Takes **O(1)**.
        4. **Push 5**: Takes **O(1)**.
        5. **Push 6**: Resizes and takes **O(4)**.
    o The total cost for 8 pushes would be:

    O(1)+O(1)+O(2)+O(1)+O(1)+O(4)+O(1)+O(1)=
    O(11)O(1) + O(1) + O(2) + O(1) + O(1) + O(4) +
    O(1)   +   O(1)   =
    O(11)O(1)+O(1)+O(2)+O(1)+O(1)+O(4)+O(1)+
    O(1)=O(11)

- The **total cost** for 8 pushes is **O(11)**.
    o The **amortized cost** per push is:

O(11)/8=O(1.375)O(11)   /   8   =
O(1.375)O(11)/8=O(1.375)

- **Amortized Cost**: Again, the **amortized cost** per operation approaches **O(1)** as more operations are performed.

Comparison with Worst-Case Analysis

Worst-case analysis examines the maximum time required for a single operation, considering the most extreme scenario. It's useful for ensuring that algorithms can handle the most challenging situations, but it doesn't necessarily reflect the **average performance** over a sequence of operations.

- **Dynamic Array Insertion**:
    - **Worst-case**: **O(n)** for each insertion (in the case of resizing).
    - **Amortized**: **O(1)** for each insertion on average, even though resizing takes **O(n)** occasionally.
- **Stack Resizing**:
    - **Worst-case**: **O(n)** when the stack resizes.
    - **Amortized**: **O(1)** on average for each push, even though resizing may occur occasionally.

Key Difference:

- **Worst-case analysis** focuses on the **maximum cost** per operation, which can be misleading when the cost is incurred only rarely (such as resizing).
- **Amortized analysis** provides a more realistic picture by taking into account the overall performance over many operations, highlighting how efficient the algorithm is on average.

Summary of Key Points:

- **Amortized analysis** is a method for analyzing the **average time complexity** of an algorithm over a series of operations, providing a more realistic measure of performance.
- **Real-world examples** like **stack resizing** and **dynamic arrays** demonstrate how expensive operations (like resizing) can be distributed across multiple operations, reducing the overall time complexity per operation.
- **Amortized time complexity** accounts for both cheap and expensive operations and gives a more accurate picture of an algorithm's efficiency.
- In contrast to **worst-case analysis**, which focuses on the **maximum time** for a single operation, **amortized analysis** reflects the **overall efficiency** of an algorithm in practical use.

- The **amortized time complexity** of operations such as array insertion or stack pushing is often **O(1)**, even though individual operations (like resizing) may take longer in certain cases.

CHAPTER 24

BIT MANIPULATION – WORKING WITH BITS EFFICIENTLY

Introduction to Bitwise Operations

Bit manipulation refers to the process of directly manipulating the individual bits of data. Since computers store information in binary format (i.e., in sequences of 0s and 1s), bit manipulation allows us to efficiently perform operations on these binary representations. Bitwise operations are some of the most **efficient** operations in computer science, as they are implemented directly in hardware and are typically faster than arithmetic operations.

Common bitwise operations include:

1. **AND (&)**: Performs a bitwise AND operation between two operands. A bit in the result is set to 1 if both corresponding bits in the operands are 1; otherwise, it is set to 0.

2. **OR (|)**: Performs a bitwise OR operation. A bit in the result is set to 1 if at least one corresponding bit in the operands is 1.

3. **XOR (^)**: Performs a bitwise XOR operation. A bit in the result is set to 1 if the corresponding bits in the operands are different.

4. **NOT (~)**: Performs a bitwise NOT operation. It inverts all the bits in the operand (also known as **bitwise complement**).

5. **Left Shift (<<)**: Shifts the bits of a number to the left, effectively multiplying it by powers of 2.

6. **Right Shift (>>)**: Shifts the bits of a number to the right, effectively dividing it by powers of 2.

Bitwise operations work at the **bit level**, which makes them extremely efficient for tasks involving low-level data manipulation and optimization.

Real-World Examples: Optimizations in Low-Level Programming, Cryptography

1. **Low-Level Programming Optimization**:
   o **Memory Efficiency**: Bitwise operations can be used for **memory-efficient storage** of flags or small integers. For example, when storing a set of **boolean flags**, instead of using one byte for each flag, multiple flags can be stored in a single byte, where each bit represents a different flag. This saves memory and speeds up access.

Example: To store the statuses of 8 boolean variables (e.g., active or inactive), you can store them in a single byte:

```text
Copy
0b10101010
```

Each bit represents the status of a different variable. To access a particular flag, you can use bitwise **AND** or **shift** operations.

Operations:

- **Set a flag**: Use the **OR** operation to set a specific bit.

```python
Copy
status |= (1 << index)   # Set bit at 'index'
```

- **Clear a flag**: Use the **AND** operation with the negation of the bit.

```python
Copy
status &= ~(1 << index)   # Clear bit at 'index'
```

233

o **Check a flag**: Use the **AND** operation.

```python
Copy
is_set = (status & (1 << index)) !=
0  # Check bit at 'index'
```

This technique is widely used in embedded systems, operating systems, and performance-critical applications.

2. **Cryptography**:

   o **XOR Operation**: The **XOR** operation is a fundamental part of many cryptographic algorithms. In particular, it is used in stream ciphers, where data is XORed with a key to encrypt or decrypt information.

Example: To **encrypt** or **decrypt** a message, you can XOR each byte of the message with a corresponding byte of the key. Since XOR is **reversible** (XORing twice with the same value will return the original), encryption and decryption are the same operation.

```python
Copy
encrypted_message = bytes([byte ^ key for
byte in message])
```

```
decrypted_message = bytes([byte ^ key for
byte in encrypted_message])   # Same as
encryption
```

The **XOR operation** is also crucial in creating **hash functions**, **checksum algorithms**, and **digital signatures**.

Common Techniques: XOR, Bit Shifts

1. **XOR (Exclusive OR)**:
   o The **XOR** operation is extremely useful for a variety of algorithms. Some of its key properties include:
      - **Self-inverse**: $a \wedge a = 0$ and $a \wedge 0 = a$.
      - **Commutative**: $a \wedge b = b \wedge a$.
      - **Associative**: $(a \wedge b) \wedge c = a \wedge (b \wedge c)$.

Applications:

   o **Swapping values without a temporary variable**:

   python
   Copy

```
a = a ^ b
b = a ^ b   # Now b is the original
value of a
a = a ^ b   # Now a is the original
value of b
```

o **Finding the single non-repeated element**: In a list of numbers where every number appears twice except for one, XOR can be used to find the number that appears once.

```python
Copy
result = 0
for num in nums:
    result ^= num
# 'result' will be the number that
appears only once
```

2. **Bit Shifts (Left Shift and Right Shift)**:

o **Left Shift (<<)**: Shifting a number's bits to the left by k positions is equivalent to multiplying the number by 2^k. Left shifts are often used for quick multiplications by powers of two.

```python
Copy
n << 1   # Equivalent to multiplying
n by 2
```

236

```
n << 2   # Equivalent to multiplying
n by 4
```

o **Right Shift (>>)**: Shifting a number's bits to the right by `k` positions is equivalent to dividing the number by 2^k and rounding down (for integer division).

```python
Copy
n >> 1   # Equivalent to dividing n by
2
n >> 2   # Equivalent to dividing n by
4
```

3. **Applications**:

o **Multiplying and Dividing by Powers of Two**: Bit shifts are extremely fast and can replace slow multiplication and division operations.

o **Extracting specific bits**: Bit shifts can be used to extract specific bits from an integer, such as checking whether a certain bit is set.

```python
Copy
bit = (n >> k) & 1   # Extract the k-
th bit from n
```

237

Applications: Memory Efficiency, Encoding

1. **Memory Efficiency**:
   - **Packing Data**: Bit manipulation is used to store multiple smaller data elements (such as flags or small integers) within a single variable. Instead of using a full byte or larger data type, you can use individual bits or groups of bits to store smaller pieces of data.

   Example: A single byte can store **8 boolean flags**. By manipulating individual bits, we can achieve **memory efficiency** without wasting space:

   ```python
   Copy
   flags = 0b00000000  # Initializing a byte
   flags |= (1 << 3)   # Set the 3rd bit to 1
   flags &= ~(1 << 3)  # Clear the 3rd bit
   ```

2. **Encoding**:
   - **Huffman Encoding**: Bit manipulation is used in **Huffman coding**, a compression algorithm that assigns variable-length codes to input characters based on their frequencies. It works by encoding characters into binary code and storing them in a compact form.

Example: In **image or video compression, bitwise operations** can be used to encode pixels or frames efficiently by minimizing the number of bits used to represent each value.

o   **Data Packing and Unpacking**: Bit manipulation is often used for efficient **data packing** and **unpacking**. For instance, in **network protocols**, data is transmitted in fixed-size packets, and bitwise operations are used to efficiently parse and construct these packets.

Example: When encoding an IP address or when constructing **bitmaps** (used for images), bitwise operations are applied to convert data to a more compact form.

Summary of Key Points

- **Bitwise operations** are powerful tools for manipulating individual bits of data. Common bitwise operations include AND, OR, XOR, NOT, and shifting.
- **XOR** is particularly useful for cryptography, data comparison, and manipulating data efficiently, while **bit**

239

shifts provide an efficient way to multiply or divide by powers of two.

- **Real-world applications** of bit manipulation include optimizing memory usage (packing data), performing cryptographic operations (encryption, XOR), and enhancing computational efficiency in low-level programming.

- **Amortized benefits** of bit manipulation include its ability to handle operations like resizing arrays or dynamically adjusting data structures while keeping time and space complexity low.

- **Applications** in **memory efficiency** (packing data into smaller units) and **encoding** (Huffman coding, data compression) make bit manipulation crucial in systems requiring high performance.

Bit manipulation is essential for systems programming, embedded systems, cryptography, and any application where performance and memory efficiency are critical.

CHAPTER 25

ADVANCED ALGORITHM DESIGN TECHNIQUES

Approximation Algorithms

Approximation algorithms are algorithms designed to find near-optimal solutions to optimization problems, especially for problems that are too complex to solve exactly within a reasonable time frame (i.e., problems that are NP-hard or NP-complete). These algorithms guarantee that the solution they provide is within a certain factor of the optimal solution.

Key Characteristics:

- **Inexact but efficient**: Approximation algorithms are typically **faster** and more **scalable** than exact algorithms but do not guarantee the optimal solution.
- **Performance guarantees**: They provide performance guarantees in terms of the **approximation ratio**, which bounds how far the solution is from the optimal solution.

Example: Traveling Salesman Problem (TSP)

- In the **Traveling Salesman Problem (TSP)**, the goal is to find the shortest possible route that visits each city once and returns to the starting city. This problem is NP-hard, and finding the exact solution takes an exponential amount of time.

- A popular approximation algorithm for TSP is the **nearest neighbor algorithm**, where the salesperson always chooses the nearest unvisited city at each step. While it doesn't guarantee the optimal solution, it can provide a **reasonably good solution** in a much shorter time.

Real-World Examples:

- **Network Routing**: In **network routing** problems, where finding the shortest path in a large network is computationally expensive, approximation algorithms like **Dijkstra's algorithm** (with heuristics) or *A search** can be used to quickly find a path that is close to optimal.
- **Machine Learning**: In **machine learning**, approximation algorithms are used for tasks like clustering or dimensionality reduction. For example, **k-means clustering** is an approximation algorithm that can quickly find a solution close to the optimal clustering of data points, even though finding the exact solution is difficult.

Randomized Algorithms and Monte Carlo Methods

Randomized algorithms utilize random numbers to influence the decision-making process, leading to algorithms that can often be more efficient than their deterministic counterparts. **Monte Carlo methods** are a subclass of randomized algorithms that rely on repeated random sampling to solve problems.

Key Concepts:

- **Randomized algorithms** do not guarantee a correct answer every time, but with high probability, they will give the correct or a near-optimal result.

- **Monte Carlo Methods** are used when the problem is too complex for exact solutions, and they provide approximate solutions by running simulations over large numbers of random samples.

Example of Randomized Algorithm: QuickSort

- **QuickSort**, a highly efficient sorting algorithm, is a classic example of a **randomized algorithm**. It picks a random element as a pivot, which helps avoid worst-case time complexity and generally improves the algorithm's performance in practice.

- **Time Complexity**: The average-case time complexity of **QuickSort** is **O(n log n)**, but its worst-case performance can be **O(n²)**. By randomly choosing the pivot, QuickSort significantly reduces the likelihood of encountering the worst-case scenario, making it very efficient on average.

Example of Monte Carlo Method: Monte Carlo Simulation for Integration

- **Monte Carlo simulations** can estimate the value of complex integrals that are difficult or impossible to solve analytically. The basic idea is to randomly sample points from the domain of the function and use the average value of the function at those points to approximate the integral.

  Example: Estimating the area under a curve (integral) using random points:

  1. Randomly generate a set of points in the domain of the function.
  2. Evaluate the function at each point and take the average.
  3. The average value of the function can then be used to approximate the area.

Real-World Examples:

- **Network Routing**: In large-scale networks, routing algorithms can use **randomization** to balance loads and find near-optimal paths in an efficient manner. **Randomized algorithms** like **random walks** can be

244

applied to problems like packet forwarding in **distributed networks**.

- **Machine Learning**: In **machine learning**, **Monte Carlo methods** are often used in **Bayesian inference** to approximate the posterior distribution when calculating exact probabilities is difficult. **Random forests** and **stochastic gradient descent** are examples of machine learning techniques that rely on randomness to improve performance.

Comparing Algorithm Design Techniques in Complex Systems

When designing algorithms for **complex systems**, choosing the right approach depends on the problem's constraints and the trade-offs between **accuracy**, **efficiency**, and **scalability**. The three key algorithm design techniques we've discussed—**approximation algorithms**, **randomized algorithms**, and **exact algorithms**—each have their strengths and are suited for different types of problems.

Approximation vs. Exact Algorithms:

- **Exact Algorithms**: Provide the optimal solution but may have exponential time complexity for complex problems (e.g., **Traveling Salesman Problem**).

- **Approximation Algorithms**: Provide a solution close to the optimal solution with guarantees on how far the solution is from optimal. They are useful for NP-hard problems where finding an exact solution is impractical (e.g., **knapsack problem**).

Trade-off: **Exact algorithms** are often only feasible for small-scale problems, while **approximation algorithms** can handle larger datasets more efficiently at the cost of precision.

Randomized Algorithms vs. Deterministic Algorithms:

- **Randomized Algorithms**: Use randomization to improve performance or handle uncertainty. They are often faster and simpler than deterministic algorithms, but they may provide incorrect results with some probability. The key is that the probability of failure is typically very low, and they often perform well on average.
- **Deterministic Algorithms**: Provide guaranteed results without randomness, making them reliable but sometimes slower or more complex than randomized alternatives.

Trade-off: **Randomized algorithms** are typically **faster** and **simpler** to implement, but they may have slight inaccuracies. On the other hand, **deterministic**

246

algorithms offer guaranteed correctness at the cost of potentially greater time complexity.

Applications in Complex Systems:

- **Network Routing**: **Randomized algorithms** can quickly find approximate solutions to routing problems in **large networks**. For example, in **distributed systems**, randomized algorithms can be used for **load balancing** and **data distribution**.
- **Machine Learning**: Many machine learning algorithms (like **stochastic gradient descent** and **random forests**) use **randomized approaches** to speed up the process of finding solutions. For very large datasets, exact methods may be impractical, so randomized methods offer a **good trade-off** between accuracy and performance.
- **Cryptography**: **Monte Carlo methods** are used in **cryptography** for probabilistic encryption and in **randomized cryptographic protocols** to improve security and efficiency.

Summary of Key Points

- **Approximation Algorithms** are used to find near-optimal solutions to NP-hard problems where finding an exact solution is computationally expensive or impractical. They are highly useful in problems like **network routing** and **machine learning**.

- **Randomized Algorithms** utilize random numbers to improve efficiency. They are particularly effective when speed is crucial, and exact solutions are not necessary. Examples include **QuickSort**, **Monte Carlo simulations**, and **stochastic methods** in machine learning.

- **Monte Carlo Methods** provide approximate solutions to problems by using random sampling and are commonly used in **simulations**, **cryptography**, and **probabilistic algorithms**.

- When comparing algorithm design techniques, the choice between **approximation**, **randomized**, and **exact algorithms** depends on the problem's complexity, desired precision, and available computational resources.

Real-World Applications:

- **Network Routing**: Randomized algorithms are widely used for packet routing, load balancing, and traffic distribution in large-scale networks.

- **Machine Learning**: Approximation and randomized algorithms power many machine learning models, especially in large-scale data processing and real-time decision-making systems.

These advanced algorithm design techniques are crucial for addressing problems in **complex systems** where exact solutions are often not feasible, and efficiency is paramount.

CHAPTER 26

ALGORITHM OPTIMIZATION – IMPROVING PERFORMANCE

Strategies for Optimizing Algorithms: Parallelism, Caching, Precomputation

Algorithm optimization is the process of improving the **performance** of algorithms to make them more efficient, faster, and scalable. Optimization can be applied at different levels, including the time complexity of operations, memory usage, and the ability to handle larger datasets. Here, we will explore three important strategies for optimization: **parallelism**, **caching**, and **precomputation**.

1. Parallelism

Parallelism refers to the practice of dividing a computational task into smaller subtasks that can be executed concurrently on multiple processors or cores. This allows the system to work on multiple parts of the problem at the same time, drastically reducing the total time required for execution.

Key Concepts:

- **Multi-core Processing**: Modern processors contain multiple cores, and algorithms can be optimized by splitting tasks into parallel threads, with each thread executed on a different core.
- **Data Parallelism**: This involves dividing data into chunks that can be processed independently in parallel.
- **Task Parallelism**: This involves dividing the tasks of the algorithm into subtasks that can be executed simultaneously.

Example:

- **Sorting Algorithms**: Algorithms like **Merge Sort** and **QuickSort** can be optimized using parallelism. For example, in **Merge Sort**, the merging of sub-arrays can be done in parallel, where different parts of the array are merged by different processors.
- **Machine Learning**: Training machine learning models, particularly deep learning models, can benefit from parallelism. The large number of matrix operations involved in training a neural network can be parallelized across multiple GPUs, speeding up the process significantly.

251

- In **databases**, queries can be optimized by parallelizing the execution of different parts of the query, such as fetching rows from different partitions of a table, or executing join operations in parallel across multiple database servers.

2. Caching

Caching is a technique where frequently accessed data is stored in a **cache** (a small, fast memory storage) to reduce the time spent fetching data from slower memory or storage systems. By storing the results of expensive function calls or database queries in a cache, subsequent requests for the same data can be served much faster.

Key Concepts:

- **Memory Cache**: Stores data in faster, smaller memory like **RAM** for quick access.
- **Disk Cache**: A storage area on the disk used to store data for faster retrieval.
- **Cache Hit vs. Cache Miss**: A **cache hit** occurs when the requested data is found in the cache, while a **cache miss**

occurs when the data is not in the cache and must be fetched from the slower storage.

Example:

- **Web Caching**: When you visit a website, resources like images, stylesheets, and JavaScript files are often cached in the browser. On subsequent visits, these resources are loaded from the browser cache rather than being fetched from the server, speeding up the loading time.
- **Database Caching**: In **databases**, caching frequently executed queries can reduce response times. For example, if a database query retrieves data from a large table, the results may be cached in **memory** to speed up future accesses.

Real-World Example: AI Processing

- In **AI processing**, especially in **deep learning** and **image recognition**, caching intermediate results (such as activations in neural networks) can significantly reduce training times. By caching results of computations, the need to recompute identical results multiple times is avoided, improving performance.

3. Precomputation

253

Precomputation involves performing calculations or processing tasks **before they are actually needed**, and storing the results for later use. This approach can be highly effective when a computation involves repetitive or expensive operations that do not change over time.

Key Concepts:

- **Memoization**: A specific form of precomputation where the results of function calls are stored in a cache so that if the function is called with the same inputs again, the result can be returned directly from the cache.
- **Lookup Tables**: Storing the results of commonly performed operations (such as trigonometric functions or factorials) in a table so that they can be retrieved quickly when needed.

Example:

- **Factorial Calculation**: Instead of calculating the factorial of a number every time it is needed, you can **precompute** and store factorials up to a certain limit in an array, allowing you to **look up** the result instantly.

```python
Copy
factorials = [1] * (max_n + 1)
for i in range(1, max_n + 1):
```

```
factorials[i] = factorials[i - 1] * i
```

- **Web Applications**: In web applications that perform expensive calculations (like image resizing), the results can be precomputed and stored. When the same image needs to be resized, it can simply be retrieved from a cache or database rather than being recomputed.

Real-World Example: AI and Machine Learning

- In **machine learning** applications, especially when training models with large datasets, certain computations (e.g., matrix multiplications, feature transformations) may be precomputed to improve efficiency during the training phase.

Memory Management Techniques

Effective **memory management** is critical for optimizing algorithms, especially when working with large datasets. Proper memory management ensures that data is stored efficiently and can be accessed quickly without overwhelming the system's resources.

Techniques for Memory Management:

1. **Garbage Collection**:
   - In high-level languages like Java or Python, **garbage collection** is responsible for automatically reclaiming memory used by objects that are no longer needed. However, in performance-critical applications, manually managing memory can help avoid the overhead of garbage collection.

2. **Memory Pooling**:
   - **Memory pooling** involves pre-allocating a pool of memory blocks, so when a memory allocation request is made, a block is quickly provided without having to request memory from the operating system each time. This reduces fragmentation and improves performance.

3. **Lazy Evaluation**:
   - **Lazy evaluation** is the process of delaying the evaluation of an expression until its value is actually needed. This can help optimize memory usage by avoiding unnecessary computations and memory allocations.

4. **In-place Operations**:
   - Performing operations in-place means modifying data directly in the same memory location rather than creating new copies of the data. For

256

example, when sorting an array, performing the sort in-place avoids the need for additional memory to store the sorted data.

Case Studies: Performance Improvement in Large-Scale Systems

1. **Optimizing Database Queries**:
   o In large-scale database systems, queries that involve multiple joins or complex aggregations can be very slow. By using **indexing**, **query optimization**, and **caching** strategies, these systems can significantly improve query performance. In databases like **MySQL** and **PostgreSQL**, indices are precomputed and stored, allowing for faster access to data.
   o **Example**: When querying a large table to fetch records based on specific criteria, a database system can optimize performance by caching frequently queried results and using indices to quickly find relevant rows.

2. **AI Processing Optimization**:
   o In machine learning systems, **batch processing**, **parallelization**, and **GPU acceleration** can be used to optimize performance. By processing

257

multiple data points simultaneously or offloading computation to specialized hardware like GPUs, machine learning algorithms can scale to handle large datasets efficiently.

o **Example**: In **training deep neural networks**, optimizing the **backpropagation algorithm** by using techniques like **mini-batch gradient descent**, **GPU parallelism**, and **model parallelism** can significantly speed up training times.

3. **Network and Cloud Systems**:

o In **cloud computing** and **distributed systems**, optimizing network communication and resource allocation can lead to significant improvements in system performance. Techniques like **load balancing**, **data replication**, and **caching** are used to ensure that services are available with minimal latency.

o **Example**: A **content delivery network (CDN)** caches static content (like images and videos) at locations close to the user, reducing the load on the server and improving access times.

258

Summary of Key Points

- **Parallelism**, **caching**, and **precomputation** are essential strategies for **optimizing algorithms** and improving their performance in real-world applications.
- **Parallelism** divides tasks into smaller subtasks that can be executed simultaneously, improving speed on multi-core systems.
- **Caching** stores frequently used data in memory, reducing the time it takes to retrieve that data in the future.
- **Precomputation** involves calculating results in advance to save time during execution, especially when results can be reused multiple times.
- **Memory management techniques** like **lazy evaluation, in-place operations**, and **garbage collection** help manage resources efficiently, which is especially critical for large-scale systems.
- Case studies show that optimization techniques are widely used in applications like **database systems, AI processing**, and **cloud computing** to improve performance.

By utilizing these optimization techniques, developers can enhance the efficiency and scalability of algorithms, ensuring their systems can handle large datasets and complex computations with minimal resource usage.

CHAPTER 27

PUTTING IT ALL TOGETHER – BUILDING REAL-WORLD APPLICATIONS

Integrating Various Data Structures and Algorithms into Practical Applications

When building real-world applications, the ability to integrate the right **data structures** and **algorithms** into the solution is crucial for achieving high performance, scalability, and reliability. In this chapter, we will discuss how to combine various algorithms and data structures in practical applications, using the example of building a **recommendation system**. We will also explore how to approach **algorithmic problem-solving** in software development and provide final thoughts on becoming an expert in **algorithmic thinking**.

Real-World Example: Building a Recommendation System

A **recommendation system** is a type of algorithm that suggests products, services, or content to users based on their preferences and behaviors. It is used in many industries, including e-commerce (Amazon, eBay), entertainment (Netflix, YouTube), and social media (Facebook, Instagram).

Step 1: Data Collection and Preprocessing

- **Data**: A recommendation system typically works with data about users and items. For instance, an **e-commerce** recommendation system might have data on products and customer interactions such as purchase history, product ratings, or browsing behavior.
- **Preprocessing**: Before applying algorithms, the data needs to be cleaned and transformed. For instance, missing values might need to be filled, categorical data might need to be encoded, and numerical features might be scaled.

Step 2: Choosing the Right Data Structures

- **Matrix Representation**: The **user-item matrix** is a key data structure in recommendation systems. This matrix represents interactions between users and items. Rows represent users, and columns represent items. Each entry in the matrix indicates how a user interacted with an item (e.g., a rating, purchase, or click).
- **Hash Maps**: A **hash map** can be used to store and retrieve data quickly. For example, you might use a hash

map to store user preferences or cached results for faster lookups.

Step 3: Algorithm Selection

The choice of algorithm depends on the type of recommendation system you are building. Below are the three main types of recommendation algorithms:

1. **Collaborative Filtering**:
   - **User-Based**: Recommend items based on similar user preferences. For example, if user A likes products X and Y, and user B likes X, we recommend Y to user B.
   - **Item-Based**: Recommend items similar to the ones the user has interacted with. For example, if user A liked item X, recommend items similar to X based on historical user data.

   Algorithm: You can use a **k-nearest neighbors (KNN)** algorithm or matrix factorization techniques like **Singular Value Decomposition (SVD)** to compute similarity scores.

2. **Content-Based Filtering**:
   - Recommend items based on their features. For example, in a movie recommendation system, you might recommend movies with similar

genres, directors, or actors to the ones the user has watched.

Algorithm: **TF-IDF** (Term Frequency-Inverse Document Frequency) can be used to represent the content features of items, and **cosine similarity** can be used to find similar items.

3. **Hybrid Approach**:
   o Combine both **collaborative filtering** and **content-based filtering** to leverage the strengths of both methods.

Algorithm: A **weighted average** of the similarity scores from both approaches or a more advanced approach like **deep learning** models (e.g., autoencoders, neural networks).

Step 4: Evaluation

- **Metrics**: Evaluate the performance of your recommendation system using metrics like **precision, recall, F1-score**, and **mean absolute error (MAE)**. Cross-validation can also be used to assess how well the system generalizes to unseen data.

How to Approach Algorithmic Problem-Solving in Software Development

In software development, algorithmic problem-solving is an essential skill. Here are some steps you can follow to tackle algorithmic problems effectively:

Step 1: Understand the Problem

- Read the problem statement carefully.
- Identify the inputs and outputs.
- Break the problem into smaller parts to understand what is being asked.

Step 2: Identify Constraints

- Consider time and space constraints, especially if the problem involves large datasets.
- Think about **edge cases** and whether the problem requires special handling for certain inputs (e.g., empty inputs, extreme values).

Step 3: Choose the Right Data Structures and Algorithms

- Select the **appropriate data structures** based on the problem. For example, if you need to search or update data efficiently, you might use a **hash table**; if the data is hierarchical, you might choose a **tree** or **graph**.

- Select an **algorithm** that is efficient given the constraints. If a problem involves finding a minimum or maximum, a **greedy algorithm** may be a good choice. If it involves optimal substructure, you might use **dynamic programming**.

Step 4: Optimize the Solution

- Look for opportunities to optimize the solution. Can you reduce the time complexity? Can you make better use of memory? Consider **amortized analysis**, **caching**, or **parallelism** to optimize the solution.

Step 5: Implement the Solution

- Write clean, readable code. Use functions to break the problem into smaller, manageable pieces.
- **Test** your implementation with various test cases, including edge cases.

Step 6: Analyze and Refactor

- After solving the problem, evaluate your solution's performance in terms of time and space complexity.
- Refactor the code to improve efficiency or readability if necessary.

Final Thoughts: Becoming an Expert in Algorithmic Thinking

Becoming an expert in **algorithmic thinking** requires both **practice** and **understanding**. Here are a few steps to improve your algorithmic thinking:

1. **Master the Fundamentals**: Understand core data structures (arrays, lists, trees, graphs, etc.) and algorithms (sorting, searching, dynamic programming, etc.). This foundation will help you recognize patterns and choose the best approaches for solving problems.

2. **Practice Regularly**: Solve problems on platforms like **LeetCode, HackerRank**, and **Codeforces**. The more problems you solve, the better you will get at identifying algorithmic patterns and applying the right algorithms efficiently.

3. **Study Algorithm Design Techniques**: Learn advanced techniques such as **divide and conquer**, **greedy algorithms**, **dynamic programming**, and **graph algorithms**. Understand the **trade-offs** between time complexity and space complexity.

4. **Analyze the Problem**: Before jumping to the code, spend time analyzing the problem. Break it down, identify patterns, and think about edge cases.

266

5. **Optimize and Refactor**: Always try to improve your solution. Can it be done in less time or with less memory? Keep optimizing as you learn new techniques.

6. **Learn from Others**: Read solutions from other experienced developers and learn different approaches to problems. This helps you expand your problem-solving toolkit.

Conclusion

In real-world applications, algorithmic problem-solving is essential to building systems that are both **efficient** and **scalable**. By integrating various data structures and algorithms, such as recommendation systems, and using strategies like **parallelism**, **caching**, and **precomputation**, developers can solve complex problems in practical ways. Becoming proficient in **algorithmic thinking** is a continuous process of practice, analysis, and learning from real-world problems. Through consistent effort, you will gain expertise and be able to tackle even the most challenging algorithmic tasks.

www.ingramcontent.com/pod-product-compliance
Lightning Source LLC
LaVergne TN
LVHW051440050326
832903LV00030BD/3173